I Knew That!

More Than 1,000 Practical Outdoor Tips
from the Readers of
FUR-FISH-GAME Magazine

Edited by Mitch Cox
Cover design by Eric R. Schweinhagen

ISBN 978-0-936622-32-3

Chapters:

I Knew That!

When our publisher Jeff Kirn suggested we start a reader tips column, I was less than enthusiastic. The best stories in the magazine already were being written by people who read *FUR-FISH-GAME* each month, and the best parts of those stories were the many practical tips, tricks and tactics, all learned from real-life experience in the outdoors.

What could a reader tips column give us that we weren't already getting? What would we do when the tipsters ran out of fresh ideas?

That was almost 20 years ago, and I am happy to say neither of those worries came to pass. The ingenuity, thrift and common sense of the people who read *FUR-FISH-GAME* never cease to amaze me. It seems there is always a better way or maybe just a more affordable way to do something. More than a thousand of those good ideas have been collected in this book, and I believe the best are absolutely ingenious.

We added an extensive index at the back so you could look up things of specific interest. Many thanks to Melissa Martin and Eric Schweinhagen. Without their diligence, this book would be far less useful.

We also broke the book down into a half-dozen broad chapters, so you can go straight to the topics that interest you most. But, really, the best way to enjoy this book is to just open to any page and start flipping through. I doubt you'll make it far before smiling to yourself and saying ... I Knew That!

– Mitch Cox, editor

Guns & Hunting

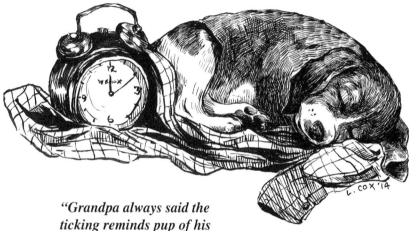

"Grandpa always said the ticking reminds pup of his mama's heartbeat."

Alarm Clock Soothes a Weaning Pup

To soothe a pup that is being weaned from his mother, roll a windup alarm clock in an old flannel shirt, one that has your scent on it, and lay it in the pup's bed. Pup will learn that your scent means "home," and the ticking clock will help lull him to sleep. Grandpa always said the ticking reminds pup of his mama's heartbeat.

Crow Call Signals Don't Spook Game

When hunting with friends, carry crow calls. A few caws make a loud and clear signal for a buddy to come to you, which is much less likely to spook game than hollering out loud in the woods.

Take a Deep Breath to Warm Up on Stand

To warm up when you must remain still on a hunting stand, take a deep breath and hold it as long as you can. Then exhale and repeat. After doing this a few times, your heart rate will increase, improving circulation, and you'll feel warmer.

Caulk Prevents Rifle Sling Strap Slipping

To prevent a gun sling slipping off your shoulder, apply a thin coat of silicone sealant caulk, work it into the strap material and allow it to cure for 24 hours. The rubbery silicone remains flexible and "tacky" enough to cling to any shirt or coat.

Minty Fresh Diaphragm Calls

Before and after hunts, I soak my diaphragm calls in mouthwash. It does a real good job of cleaning them and also gives them a fresh, minty taste.

Turn Closet into Gun Cabinet with Locking Doorknob

Turn a closet into a large-capacity gun cabinet by installing a locking doorknob. Not as secure as a safe, but for less than $10, you can keep every firearm you own under lock and key.

Edible Arrow Grease

To prevent hunting arrow broadheads rusting, coat with corn oil pan spray. It works great and is 100-percent edible should the arrow pass through a deer.

Clean Deer Cavity with Vinegar Water

When I get a field-dressed deer home, I mix 1/2-cup vinegar with 2 gallons warm water. Then, using an old terry cloth towel, I thoroughly wash out the inside of the deer. Vinegar and water clean the meat without adding any unwanted flavor.

Use a Turkey Box to Call Squirrels

The "cutting" side of a turkey box can be used to call squirrels. They may come running to check out the loud, sharp sounds. At the very least, curious squirrels up a tree may look and expose themselves for a shot.

Play a Raccoon Tune on the Harmonica

I carry a harmonica when coon hunting. If I am unable to locate a treed coon, I blow the harmonica a few times at different pitches. A coon will almost always take a look, which enables me to shine its eyes. I also play the harmonica to pass the time while waiting for the hounds to strike a track.

Washers Work as Stump-Shooting Arrow Stoppers

Before stump shooting with bow and arrow, put a small washer between the field tip and the arrow shaft. It has little effect on flight but makes it much easier to pull the arrow from a stump.

Ladder Handy for One-Man Deer Loading

When hunting alone, I tie a short section of ladder to my car's rooftop rack. If I get a deer, I wrap the deer in a tarp; pull down the ladder; tie the deer to the ladder; then easily lift one end and slide ladder and deer up onto the car-top carrier. Can also be used to load a deer into the back end of a pickup truck.

Use Old Bedspread Batting for Snow Camo

As snow camo for hunting geese, I use the batting from an old bedspread. Geese have very poor depth perception. I just sit on a white 5-gallon bucket covered poncho-style with the batting. If you must buy it new, it can be found at fabric outlet stores for about $1 a yard.

Hornet Nest Paper Patch for Muzzleloaders

Locate an inactive hornet nest and salvage the outer layer. Then, when you charge your muzzleloader with the usual measured powder charge, tamp it and seat a patch of the hornet paper before you seat the patched ball or conical bullet. Makes a natural moisture barrier and cap guard.

Straight-Arrow Tester Tool

A slightly bent shaft can throw an arrow off course. For under $5, I built a tool to determine arrow trueness. To each end of a 14-inch board, I attached the rollers from a roller-type cabinet door catch. Now, I simply lay an arrow on the rollers and slowly spin. Any wobble may be seen instantly.

Black-Powder Primer Flow Control

To prevent fine-grain 4F priming powder always leaking, clean out a plastic glue bottle, the kind with a twist top, and use that for carrying and pouring the fine powder. No powder spillage, and the bottle is airtight, too.

Serrated Shears Ideal for Field Dressing

The serrated-edge shears used by rescue workers to cut away seat belts make the ultimate small-game and bird-cleaning tool. They easily snip through hide and nip off feet, paws and heads. They also do an excellent job opening an abdomen without puncturing internal organs.

Make a Shooting Bipod from Aluminum Arrows

A lightweight shooting bipod can be made from two aluminum arrows, a small bolt and nut. Drill and then bolt the shafts together just in front of the fletching (rubber fletching will protect the gunstock). Leave field points on the opposite ends, and the bipod won't slip even on frozen ground. It should be the right height for shooting from the sitting position, and a second set can be cut down for the prone position.

Quick-Draw Holster for Turkey Box Call

A belt holster for a box call may be fashioned easily from a 10-by-14-inch piece of short-nap carpet. Roll the carpet, nap side in, around the call with about a 3-inch lap. Hand-sew it together and then close the bottom by stitching straight across. Sew on a wide belt loop through the lapped area. If you use carpet with an earth-tone backing, you can camouflage by simply streaking with gray, green or tan paint. The carpet "sets" around the call's shape for secure carry, yet the call can be quickly drawn and reholstered with one hand.

Door Spring Brings Turkey Decoys to Life

To make collapsible turkey decoys more lifelike, separate the two-part stake and insert a small piece of door spring (available at hardware stores). In even a slight breeze, the decoy will bob, giving it a more active appearance. Paint the eyeballs with glossy black paint (model paint works) to take away the dead look.

DIY Turkey Trophy Display

To display a turkey beard, save that empty shell that fired the fatal shot. Preserve the beard by packing the skin end in salt until it is good and dry. Punch the primer out of the shell; tie a knot in one end of a 12-inch length of rawhide lace and slide this through the shell and out the primer hole. Snug the knot to the hole and then fill all but 1/4-inch of the shotshell with latex or silicone caulk sealer. Now, push the skin end of the dried beard into the shotshell until sealer oozes out around the edges. Allow sealer to dry for a day then trim the excess. Tie a loop in the rawhide, and your trophy is ready to hang on the wall.

Dog Choker Chain Doubles as Gambrel

A dog's chain choker collar can be hung from a rafter or tree limb and used as a skinning gambrel. Just place a foot in the noose-like loop, and the harder you pull, the tighter it grips. A length of rope can be added to the other end to easily adjust hanging height.

Store Diaphragm Game Calls in the Refrigerator

Store used diaphragm calls in the refrigerator to keep the latex soft and pliable.

Preventing Rust in the Gun Cabinet

To help prevent firearms rusting in the gun cabinet, cut a small sponge to fit in a clean tuna can, pour lite gun oil on the sponge and place the can at the bottom of the cabinet. The vapor lightly coats the guns and inhibits rust. Place paper items in the cabinet in a sealed plastic bag.

Inner Tube Scope Covers

To make a handy scope cover, simply cut a cross section out of an old truck tire inner tube to make a big, wide rubber band. Slip one end over the eyepiece then stretch it over the other end.

Ironing Out Arrow Vanes

Straighten warped or rippled plastic arrow vanes with a clothes iron on the lowest setting. Fold a thin cloth over the vane, lay flat on ironing board and apply light pressure for only a few seconds, making passes over the vane. Check after every pass to make sure too much heat is not being applied. Much easier than removing the old and gluing on new vanes.

Whiten Rifle Sights for Better Visibility

Dab a little white correction fluid on the back of a rifle sight's front blade and it will be easier to see in low light or when hunting at night with a light. Simply scrape off with a fingernail to return the sight to the original dark color.

Handy Oiled Rags Keep Gun Rust Under Control

Where gun metal is touched it may discolor or rust, so I keep a lightly oiled rag in a sealed plastic bag in my gun cabinet, one in my gun case, one in the 5-gallon bucket I use to carry things when trap shooting, and one in each of the 5-gallon buckets I use when hunting. With oily rags so handy, it takes just a moment to wipe off the fingerprints and keep the metal looking like new.

Long-Lasting Oak Camo for the Tree Stand

In late summer, cut oak limbs (about finger thick) that have a lot of green leaves on them and wire these around your tree stand to camouflage it. The limbs will not drop their leaves until well after hunting season and still will be up there helping you hide when other trees are bare.

Prevent Fletching Cement Drying in Tube
To prevent arrow-fletching cement drying in the neck of the tube, I thread a needle with a 6-inch piece of thread, stick the needle down the tube opening into the cement and then put the cap back on. The needle prevents air reaching and drying the cement; the thread allows for easy retrieval of the needle; and the cap keeps everything in place.

Cordless Drill Eases Tree Step Installation
Use a battery-powered cordless drill to make pilot holes before installing tree steps. The drill is quiet, easy to carry, and the pilot holes make it much easier to screw steps into the tree trunk.

Roll Old Carpet for a Free Archery Target
Use old carpeting as a backstop for archery practice. A large piece rolled over three times (carpet side in) then folded in half and tied with a rope stops all target arrows and most hunting broadheads. Paint targets right on the carpet.

Hook, Line & Sinker Tree Stand Retriever Line
File the barbs off a No. 2 treble hook, tie it on a long length of heavy fishing line, press on a couple of split shot sinkers, and wind the whole thing up on a short pencil. It fits into a pill bottle and works like a charm for hooking and retrieving the things that fall out of a tree stand.

Reeling In the Downed Ducks
When hunting ducks without a retrieving dog, bring a rod and reel with a top-water bass plug. Cast the plug over a downed duck, snag it, and reel it in.

Fingernail Polish Keeps Your Powder Dry
Before black-powder hunting in damp weather, apply clear fingernail polish to seal the joint where the cap seats on the rifle. Also seal the joint where the nipple threads meet the tang. Dries

in seconds, keeps moisture out, and you will never lose a cap.

Let Your Deer Lure Blow in the Wind
Put deer lure on the seeds in a milkweed pod, let it dry and then store in a plastic bag. When up in a tree stand hunting, take out the pod, add a couple of more drops of fresh scent, pull out a few of the seeds and let them float to the ground. This shows wind direction and also creates a nice scent trail. After about 20 minutes, release more.

Field Dress with a Belt Hatchet or Small Axe
A belt hatchet or small axe is ideal for splitting a deer's pelvic bone and breastplate, much easier and safer than using a knife.

Window Cleaner "Dry Cleans" a Muzzleloader
Window cleaner cleans and shines a black-powder rifle without any of the rust that water may cause.

Clean Taxidermy Mounts with Snowballs
Wipe taxidermy mounts with snowballs to remove dust and dirt without making everything wet.

Drywall Knife Great for Hunting
A drywall knife that uses a replaceable, retracting blade becomes an excellent gutting and skinning knife when you replace the straight blade with the hook-type shingle/tile blade. The razor-sharp curved blade outperforms any straight hunting knife.

Wild Game Frozen Food
To freeze rabbits, squirrels, doves or quail, cut a 3-inch hole in the top of a gallon milk jug leaving the handle on. Put the cleaned game in the container, fill with water, mark the date and kind of game on the outside of the jug, and then freeze. The meat lasts longer with no freezer burn.

Make Field Decoys from Cardboard Boxes
Duck or goose field decoys can be made from cardboard boxes.

Just trace the bodies on the corners and cut out with a sharp knife. Cut out heads from whatever cardboard is left, attach and paint all to waterproof.

Lightly Oiled Gloves Prevent Gun Rust
To ward off fingerprints and surface rust, wear a pair of jersey or cotton gloves whenever cleaning or handling firearms, and spray a little gun oil on the palms.

Corrugated Cardboard Protects Knife Edge

Protect the blade edge of a stored knife with a "sheath" cut out of a corrugated cardboard box.

To protect the blade edge of a knife that doesn't have a sheath, cut a piece out of a corrugated cardboard box wider and longer than the blade itself and then slowly slide the blade into the middle, between the solid outside surfaces. The corrugated part should hold the blade securely. Just be aware that while the cardboard protects the blade, it doesn't protect you. Any sharp blade can easily slice through cardboard, so handle with care.

Use a Sawzall to Quarter Big Game
Instead of using a hand meat saw to quarter big game, I use a Sawzall with the 12-inch wood-cutting blade. It quickly does a neat, clean job with much less effort.

Polident® Cleans Mouth Calls, Too
To keep mouth diaphragm calls clean, dissolve half of a Polident tablet in 8 ounces of water and then soak the calls for about 5 minutes. It doesn't hurt them. Take the calls out and place toothpicks between the latex layers to dry.

Store Bore Brush in the Original Pack
Keep gun cleaning bore brushes in the original hard plastic package. Just cut the top out and then hang the card on a wall. Stored this way, you can read the caliber size off of the package.

Instant Snow Decoys

To convert Canada geese decoys into snow geese, fill a coffee can half full of plaster of Paris then fill the rest with rubbing alcohol. Thoroughly mix, and you have a temporary paint. Paint solid for snow geese; splash and splotch for blue geese. A hosing will wash the decoys clean again.

Tie Deer for Easier Dragging

Before dragging a deer from the woods, make a cut through the lower jaw at the point of the "V," push a rope through this hole from inside the mouth, tie to one front foot between hoof and dewclaw, and then loop rope around and tie up the other leg. Tied this way, the hooves stay tucked up under the chin for easier dragging with fewer hang-ups.

Panty Hose Preserves Birds for Taxidermy

To preserve a duck or pheasant for taxidermy, slide it into old panty hose. Just smooth and slide the bird in headfirst. When you get home, cut off the foot of the stocking and slide the bird on out that end.

Old Alarm Clock Makes a Poor Man's Trail Timer

Wedge a cheap battery-powered clock against a tree. Take out the battery, tie a string around it, and then place it back in the clock. Run the string across the trail and secure it on the other side. When the string is tripped, the battery comes out and the clock stops, telling you when it happened.

Recycle Fake Christmas Trees as Camo for Blind

Recycle old artificial Christmas trees by attaching the branches to a permanent hunting blind. Breaks up the shape, looks natural and lasts for years.

Make a Squirrel Call from a Stove Bolt and Jar Lid

A squirrel call can be made with a jar lid and a stove bolt. Cup the lid in one hand with the top against your palm. Draw the bolt threads across the edge of the lid while opening and closing the hand holding the lid. Quick rasping makes a sound like a barking squirrel. Try this with different sized lids and bolts until you find a combination that sounds just right.

Seeing the Sights
To increase low-light visibility with iron sights, dab a little white-out product on the front bead and then paint a "V" on the rear sight. You can remove it whenever you want with a fingernail.

Insulated Seat Pads Keep Toes Toasty, Too
When stand hunting in winter, bring two insulated seating pads. Sit on one and put the other under your feet to keep toes warm.

Make Decoys Unsinkable with Spray Foam Insulation
To make decoys leak-proof (if not bulletproof), fill with the expanding foam sealant used for insulation purposes. Drill a hole in the top of the decoy's head and one near the tip of the tail. Insert the tube from the can of sealant and fill until foam exits the other hole.

Old Frisbees Great for Shotgun Practice
Used Frisbees make great flying targets for shotgun practice. They leave no residue when hit, cost next to nothing at garage sales (I never pay more than a dime) and need no mechanism to launch. You can even toss your own with a little practice.

Gas Torch Tip Brush Cleans Muzzleloader Nipples
A gas torch tip cleaning brush is ideal for cleaning the nipple of a muzzleloader. The brushes come in different sizes and easily bend to fit the nipples in most guns.

Use Cedar Bedding for a Clothing Cover Scent
For natural-smelling hunting clothing, use the inexpensive pet bedding made from the shavings of red cedar trees. The plastic bag typically has holes in it to release the cedar smell while still containing the shavings. For extra scent, just squeeze the bag a couple of times.

Button Holds Rifle Sling on Shoulder

To prevent rifle slings sliding off during carry, sew a large button on top of the shoulder of your hunting coat.

Add a Sock to Hold Scent on Dog Training Bumper

Plastic dog training bumpers don't retain scent very well. To remedy this, pull an old but clean cotton sock over the dummy before applying the scent on the sock. Changing scents is as easy as changing socks, but do wash the dummy between changes, to avoid confusing the dog.

Dove Decoys Calm Skittish Deer

Hang a pair of dove decoys next to your tree stand to put skittish deer at ease. Live doves don't hang around people that way.

Hang Turkey Decoy to Prevent Wrinkling

If a foam turkey decoy is folded for storage, the wrinkles can become permanent. Instead, store in the open position. Bend a wire coat hanger to fit, insert this hanger into the opening of the decoy body, and then use it to hang the decoy upside down from a ceiling hook.

Carry .22 Cartridges in a Coin Purse

Coin purses work great for carrying .22 cartridges. They stay readily available yet are not gathering lint, etc., in the bottom of a pants pocket. The vinyl oval ones with the slit across the top that pinch open hold a dozen or so cartridges. The bigger ones that snap shut hold many more.

Bore Sight a Bolt-Rifle with One Shot

To bore-sight a scope on a bolt-action rifle with just one shot, remove the bolt and place the gun on sandbags. Set a target with a 6-inch black bull's-eye at 100 yards and look at it through the barrel. Move the rifle to center the bull in the barrel. Without moving the barrel, look through the scope and adjust it until the crosshairs also line up on the bull. Keep checking and adjusting. When the bull is centered in the barrel and also in the scope crosshairs, the first shot fired should hit the bull or come close.

Sheet Plastic Makes an Instant Goose Field Blind

Instead of digging field pits for goose hunting, use a piece of heavy-duty clear plastic sheeting, maybe 25 by 50 feet. Anchor the edges with rocks and decoys. Get underneath, except for your head, and lie on a separate piece of plastic with a boat cushion under your head. Now place a decoy near your head to help disguise any motion. From the air, it looks to the birds like a big puddle. If it gets a little dirty, it works even better.

Mouse Pads Make Handy Handgun Mats

Companies often give away computer mouse pads with the company names on them, and these freebies make fine pistol mats, protecting the finish while the gun is in a drawer, etc. They also may protect a tabletop when you clean the gun.

Use Rope to Rattle Antlers on the Ground

When bowhunting in a tree stand, don't rattle antlers up in the tree. Instead, tie the antlers to parachute cord and lower them to the ground. Now use the cords like puppet strings to make them rattle. With a little practice, you can make very realistic sounds with very little movement up in the tree. Any deer coming in stays focused at ground level, and this is especially effective with a deer decoy out in front.

Easier Tree-Step Cranking

The knurled portion of screw-in tree steps can be tough on hands and gloves. Once a step is started, I slide a 4-inch length of thick-walled 3/4-inch PVC pipe over the knurled portion and use it as a free-turning sleeve while cranking in the step.

Muzzleloader Percussion Cap Tin Also Holds Patches

Empty muzzleloader percussion cap tins are handy for carrying lubed or solvent-soaked patches when hunting. They stay moist and clean, and placing the tin in an inside pocket assures a water-based solvent won't freeze even during winter hunts.

Make a Scent Drag with Felt Weather Strip

A deer hunting scent drag can be made by cutting felt weather stripping to the desired length, poking a hole in the center, and tying it on to a stout string. Also works for hanging scent at stands, scrapes and mock scrapes.

Make Snap Caps with Spent Cartridges

Even though today's guns can take a lot of dry firing, snap caps still should be used. Make your own by removing the primers from spent cartridges and filling the primer pockets with hot glue. Trim off the excess, and start practicing.

Make a Crow Decoy with a Hanger and Sock

To quickly make an effective crow decoy, bend a wire coat hanger into a crow silhouette and pull a black sock over it. Bend the hook out straight, and you can push it into the ground or into the top of an old fence post to secure the decoy.

Newspaper in Bag Makes Warm, Dry Ground Seat

When deer hunting, I place a folded newspaper inside a plastic garbage bag and carry it in my daypack. It works as an insulated seat on cold, damp ground, and I have a ready supply of dry paper should I want to make a fire.

Keep a Dime with Your Scope

To always have a dime handy for adjusting a scope's setting dials, place one on the top adjusting dial, put the cap back on, and then screw down tight.

Cap Sharp Tree Step Points with Wire Nuts

When storing or carrying screw-in tree steps, cap the sharp tips with the wire nuts used to connect electrical wires in junction boxes. They come in a variety of sizes, one of which should securely screw onto any tip.

Fishing Reel Makes a Mini Hoist for Tree Stand

To always have a convenient winch for hauling gear up and

down out of tree stands, fill an old fishing reel with 20-pound-test line and put it in your pack.

Noon Siren a Great Coyote Locator Call
When the noon siren goes off in a rural town, the local coyotes usually answer. Simply be within earshot when it happens, and you should be able to locate the coyotes that howl back. Train whistles have the same effect.

Shovel Helps Locate Arrows that Miss Target
Arrows that slide under the grass may be found by sliding a round-nose shovel along on its side edge. Go back and forth across the suspected arrow path, applying light down pressure until you feel the shovel slide up and over the arrow shaft.

Homemade High-Vis Targets
High-visibility foam-board rifle targets make it easy to see where shots hit. I make my own by placing orange stick-on target dots on thick foam plastic picnic plates.

Drop a Skunk at Your Stand for Natural Cover Scent
Place a road-killed skunk near your stand and it will help cover your scent even when the wind blows the wrong way.

Make Your Own Ghillie Suit
Achieve a 3-D effect by sewing silk-flower foliage onto an old camouflage outfit. Lifelike oak, maple and fern leaves may be found at craft stores. The stems are reinforced with plastic or wire, which holds the shape even when wet.

Muzzleloader Ramrod Holder
To prevent a muzzleloader ramrod slipping out, check to see if the rod is threaded on both ends. Most are. If so, find a screw that matches the threads and saw off the head, leaving 1 inch. Screw this into the ramrod, leaving about 1/2-inch protruding. Now, drill a hole where the ramrod end sits flush against the rifle's wood stock. Put epoxy in the hole and then turn the cut-off screw

into this hole. After the epoxy dries the screw won't back out, and with a couple of quick turns, you can screw the ramrod onto the part of the screw that protrudes.

Hair Spray for Arrow Feathers
Hair spray will keep feather arrow vanes dry and stiff.

Camo for Eyeglass Glare
To prevent the glare from eyeglasses spooking turkeys and other game, glue a small section of camo netting to the underside bill of your hunting cap and let it hang down.

Always Use Rubber Butt Pads
A rubber butt pad should be installed on all long guns, even rimfire .22 rifles. The pad not only reduces felt recoil but also helps to hold the butt in place on your shoulder while shooting. If the gun should be stood in a corner, the rubber pad may keep it from slipping and falling to the floor.

Removing a Stuck Muzzleloader Ramrod
Cut a patch too big or let one get too fouled while cleaning a muzzleloader, and the ramrod may get stuck. To twist it free without marring the rod, use the pliers designed to pull wires off auto spark plugs. The jaws are rounded and padded.

Don't Bug-Spray Your Gun
Set your gun well upwind before spraying yourself with bug repellent. The spray can damage the finish, eventually giving it an unsightly, pitted look.

Old School Gun Cabinet
An old school locker makes a good gun cabinet. They are made of steel, there is room for long guns and a top shelf for handguns and ammo, and the door handle is designed for a lock.

Fixing Arrow Feathers
To bring feather arrow fletchings back to shape, place over a

steaming teapot for a few seconds and then smooth with fingers.

Recycle Election Signs as Practice Targets
After an election, the signs that are left behind cluttering the roadways may be collected and used as free-standing target holders for rifle or handgun practice (especially the ones promoting anti-gun candidates).

Use Chalk Line to Flush Squirrels
When hunting squirrels, carry a carpenter's chalk-line box (but with no chalk in it). When a squirrel is treed, tie the line to brush then move to the opposite side of the tree, reeling out line as you go. A tug on the line shakes the brush and spooks the squirrel around to your side of the tree for a shot. The line is reeled back in, and the box goes back on your belt.

Check Muzzleloader Before Loading
Before loading a muzzleloading gun, fire just a cap at a leaf on the ground. If the leaf moves, the barrel and nipple are clear for loading. When you must transport a loaded muzzleloader, remove the cap or priming powder and lower the hammer onto a piece of red cloth. The red cloth reminds you the gun has a charge in it and also protects the nipple.

Mark Trees for Stands with Electrical Tape
When you find a nice tree for a stand, mark it with a wrap of black electrician's tape. It stays on for years, unseen unless you are looking for it, and because the tape is somewhat reflective, you can find it in the dark with a flashlight.

Undercoat Squeaky Tree Stand
Auto undercoating (costs $3) will quiet a squeaky tree stand and also deaden contact noises. Just paint right over the finish. The black blends about as good as camo, and it resists rusting, too.

Check Wind with Baking Soda in Eye Drop Bottle
Fill a squeeze eye drop bottle with baking soda to make a handy

wind detector. Turn the bottle upside-down and give it a squeeze. Baking soda is so light it reveals even the lightest breeze.

Put Choke Tube in a Pill Bottle
Pill bottles are ideal for storing screw-in choke tubes. Write the gauge, choke, and make of gun on a label then tape it to the bottle. Do the same thing with cleaning brushes and jags.

Free Gun Rust-Busters
To prevent guns rusting, take the little packets out of shoe boxes or new electronics (the ones that say "silica gel, do not eat") and put them in the gun case. They absorb moisture out of the air. Every so often replace the old with new.

Campfire Provides Free Face Camo
Crush a piece of wood charcoal from a spent campfire into a plastic bag, seal and save to be used as face camo during hunting season. Cleans up with soap and water.

Predator Call Good for Crows, Too
A rabbit-in-distress predator call works great for crows, too. The crows come in to mob what they think is tearing the rabbit to pieces—and you never know when a real fox or coyote may come in for a closer look.

Go to Water to Pick Up Lost Blood Trail
If you lose a blood trail near a stream, mark the last good sign and then walk the banks in the surrounding area. Wounded animals go to water, and if an animal will lose blood anywhere, it will be while climbing the bank. Rule of thumb for our area is an animal hit on one side of the river is usually recovered on the other.

Use Candle Wax to Keep Your Powder Dry
To keep the powder charge in a percussion muzzleloader dry, light a small candle and let the wax drip over the cap and nipple. The wax seals out moisture, but the cap still fires on impact.

One-Man Deer Loading

To load a big deer in a pickup truck without help, throw a rope over a stout tree limb, tie one end to the rear bumper and the other around the deer's neck. Drive the truck forward to pull deer up to the limb and tie off the rope. Now back the truck under the deer, untie the rope and lower it.

Recycle Hip Boots into Waterproof Ground Seats

Have a pair of hip boots ready for the garbage? Cut a 12-inch square out of the side with the belt strap and you have a nice, lightweight, waterproof seat that is ideal for wet-weather hunting. Use the belt strap attachment, and when you get up, it goes with you.

Knock, Knock Squirrel Call

When squirrel hunting, carry a dry walnut shell in your pocket. When the squirrels are not moving around much, tap the shell on your gun's wood buttstock. The squirrels will come out to investigate the intriguing sound.

Roughen Leather Sling for a Better Grip

To keep a leather rifle sling from slipping off your shoulder, use a sharp knife to lightly roughen up the polished top-grain leather on the inner side of the sling.

Hand in Glove Deer Dragging

Tight-fitting cotton gloves with the gummy rubber on the palms and fingers are ideal for dragging a deer out of the woods. With very little grip pressure you can hang onto an antler or leg, reducing hand and arm fatigue.

Feather "Windicator" for the Bow

Use waxed dental floss to tie and dangle a downy feather from your bowstring. The light feather will pick up the lightest breeze, is always visible at a glance, and won't affect arrow flight.

Use House Wrap for a Warm & Ducky Blind

To make a duck blind warmer and more windproof, use the wrap contractors use when siding a house. Most contractors have scrap pieces, and it doesn't take much. The wrap I use is green and works very well. Tack it to the floor and around the inside walls. You will be amazed at the difference.

Recycle Burlap Feed Bags to Make Easy Blinds

Old burlap feed bags can be ripped open, dyed or painted camo patterns to make easy hunting blinds. Or just wrap one around your legs when seated to better blend in with the ground cover and also stay a little warmer.

Notch a Paddle for Easier Decoy Recovery

Cut a notch in the edge of a boat paddle, and when it is slipped under a duck decoy, the notch will catch the cord so you can lift the decoy into the boat. Keeps hands dry and also lessens the rocking caused by leaning over the side.

Check Old Buttstocks for Hidden Treasure

Always remove the butt plate or pad and look inside the buttstock of a second-hand rifle or shotgun. You never know what a previous owner may have stashed in there. Some old-timers would place a roll or two of dimes in the stock to dampen recoil and also serve as a little emergency cash.

Wet Squirrels & Rabbits Before Skinning

Before skinning a rabbit or squirrel, dip it in water to help keep the hair from getting on the meat. Also look under the skinned armpits for waxy balls about the size of a pea. Remove them because they can give the meat a bad taste.

Static-Free Dryer Sheet Works on Reloader, Too

If static buildup causes the powder to cling to the plastic drop tube or funnel while you are reloading, wipe it down with one of those static-free fabric softener sheets used in clothes dryers.

Long John Turkey Bag

Cut the legs off old long johns to make turkey carry bags that hold the wings and tail feathers securely in place.

Butcher Deer Over a Wheelbarrow for Easy Cleanup

When you hang a deer for butchering, line a wheelbarrow with a plastic sheet and park it underneath then butcher as you normally would. When you're done, tie up the plastic and discard. You won't even have to wash out the wheelbarrow.

Bow & Arrow Sighting Tip

Before sighting in a bow, number the test arrows with a marker. If an arrow is always off, it may be the arrow and not the bow.

Combination Walking Stick Handgun Rest

Cut a hardwood walking stick about 6-1/2 feet long with a fork at the top, and it may also serve as a handgun rest for taking tree shots at squirrels. Leave stubs at strategic places when cutting off branches lower down the stick, to rest the handgun while taking lower shots.

Clothes Iron Removes Dings from Gun Stocks

To remove small dings from a wood rifle stock, place a damp towel over the ding and place a hot clothes iron on the towel. Slowly rock back and forth. The heat will raise the dented wood, usually enough to sand and refinish.

Spray Muzzleloader Patch with Cooking Oil

When a muzzleloader bore gets dirty, spray cooking oil on a patch, run it down the barrel and follow with a dry patch. Makes loading easier, improves accuracy, and also seasons the bore.

Build a Better Bird & Bunny Brush Pile

To make better brush piles for birds and bunnies, first lay down some wood pallets and then pile the brush on top. Creates perfect hiding places under the brush, and the old skids may be had for the asking at most receiving docks.

Hidden Tag Identifies Your Gun
Mark guns in case they are lost or stolen by removing the butt plate and placing a small tag with your name and phone number between the stock and this plate. Trap tags work great. If you don't have any, scratch your name and address on a piece of aluminum pie plate. Or insert a sealed plastic bag holding a small piece of paper with your name, address and phone number.

Spray Paint Crow Decoys for Lifelike Shine
Spray old crow decoys with clear, high-gloss Krylon paint (other paints also work) to make them shine like real crow feathers.

Styrofoam Pellets Fill Lightweight Shooting Bags
Instead of putting sand in shooting bags, fill with Styrofoam packing pellets. The bags are stable yet much easier to carry.

Whistle to Stop Running Deer
To stop a running deer for a shot, whistle as loud as you can. If you can't whistle loudly on your own, hang a piercing whistle around your neck.

BB Shot Best for Wounded Ducks
When duck hunting, bring some BB shells. When a wounded bird is swimming away, a load of BB in the rear finishes the duck without damaging any breast meat.

Strap-On Tree Step Doubles as Rifle Rest
Strap-on tree climbing steps can be strapped onto almost any tree in seconds to provide a rock-steady shooting rest. Use a rubber-coated step and you won't mar the finish on the forend stock.

Wrap Your Rifle with Livestock Bandage Tape
To camouflage a scope and rifle barrel, wrap it with stretchable livestock bandaging tape. It comes in brown, black and white, adheres only to itself, leaves no residue, and is reusable. A 5-yard

roll costs about $1.50.

Use Jar Lid Opener to Pull Arrows from Targets
For an easier time pulling arrows out of targets, use one of those rubber jar lid openers to get a secure grip on the shafts.

Use an Old Gun Case as a Car Tool Box
Keep your car's road tools in an old gun case in the trunk. Then, if you ever pick up a hunter in the field, you will have a way to legally carry the firearm. Could save a citation.

Old Camera Bag Makes Great Shooter's Bag
A large camera bag is ideal for packing shooting supplies to the range. Such bags are always cheap at thrift stores, lightweight and padded with a comfortable shoulder carry strap and more than enough compartments to keep everything organized.

Store Hunting Clothes in Bark Mulch
Put a couple of inches of dry bark mulch (comes in pine, hemlock, and cedar at the local garden store) in the bottom of the plastic tub where you store hunting clothes. The clothes will have a "woodsy" smell when you bring them back out next season.

Paper Towel Helps Keep Flintlock Powder Dry
To keep a flintlock firing in wet weather, wad a little paper towel and put it in the powder pan with the frizzen down, holding it in place. The paper absorbs moisture, keeping it out of the touchhole and powder charge.

Bee-Proof Your Blind with Pest Strips
To help prevent hornets or wasps taking over an enclosed hunting blind during the off-season, hang plenty of no-pest strips. They catch and kill flying insects up to four months.

Low-Cost Surplus Scent Suits
Save a bundle on "scent-blocking" hunting clothes by buying chemical suits at the Army surplus store. They are lined with

scent-absorbing charcoal, and sealed in the original bag typically only cost $15-$30. They come in all sizes, in drab green and woodland camouflage.

Homemade 12-Gauge Snap Cap
Make a 12-gauge snap cap from a fired shell and a No. 2 pencil. Use a punch to remove the spent primer from the shotshell. Now squeeze the pencil eraser into the primer well and cut it off even with the bottom of the cartridge. The eraser cushions the impact of the firing pin to prevent damage when dry-firing.

Get a Leg Up on Easier Skinning
After hanging a deer to skin, tie one of the legs to a nearby tree or a stake in the ground. This stops the deer from spinning while you are skinning it.

Record Yourself Calling for a Sound/Reality Check
Record yourself while game calling, and then replay it. You may be amazed by how different you sound from how you think you sound. Practice will improve the weak areas.

Recycle Burlap Feed Sacks for Arrow Targets
To make a target for field-point arrows, fill a burlap feed sack with stretch wrap, trash bags, grocery bags, or any plastic of the type. Keep packing the bag tight with your knees as you fill it up. When it is full, stitch the top using a nail and string or duct tape it shut. Draw a target circle right on the bag. Stops the fastest arrow, and it can be pulled back out with thumb and fingers.

Lay Bags Lengthwise for Straighter Shooting
When shooting off sandbags, turn them lengthwise instead of shooting across them to give the rifle more contact support.

Light Sticks Help Track Deer After Dark
Keep a pack of light sticks (sold at camping supply stores) in your deer hunting pack. Should you have to trail a deer after dark, use them to mark the hit site, the blood trail when it becomes

difficult to follow, or last blood. Really speeds the process when you need to circle and pick up the trail again.

Party Balloon Plumps Up Collapsible Turkey Decoy
Party balloons keep collapsible foam turkey decoys plump. Just blow up the balloon to the desired size and stick it in the decoy.

Lego® Light Glow Gun Sight
Use a glow stick from a Lego set to make a glowing fiber-optic front gun sight. Cut to fit and use J.B. Weld to hold it in place. Costs almost nothing and works great.

Plastic Bag on the Muzzle Catches Gun Cleaning Mess
To control the mess when scrubbing the bore of a gun, attach a gallon-size plastic zip-lock bag to the muzzle with a rubber band. Catches the solvent splatter from the bore brush, and when you're through, just leave dirty patches, rags, etc., in the bag and toss in the trash.

Wounded Deer Head Upwind, Too
Before trailing a wounded deer, check the wind direction. After the initial burst, the deer will not stay long in your downwind scent trail. If you lose the trail, keep this in mind and you may be able to find it again.

Carpet Muffles Creaky Tree Stand
While building a permanent tree stand, insert strips of old carpet at the wood-to-wood and wood-to-tree contact points to eliminate the loud creaks that can spook wary deer.

Extra-Long Shooting Bags
Make extra-long shooting bags by cutting the legs off old jeans. Sew one end shut, fill with sand or another fill material and tie the other end shut.

3-D Archery Target Patch
Patch the shot-out area on a 3-D archery target with insulating

foam—the type made for sealing window and door frames that comes in a spray can. Once it's cured, you can trim with a utility knife and paint to match rest of target (if you want).

Single-Pack Wet Wipes Ideal for Field Dressing
The single-pack "wet wipes" given away at restaurants are great for cleaning up after field dressing game. They stay moist because you only open the ones you use. Carry a dozen or so in your pack along with folded paper towel.

Electrical Wire Clears a Jammed Bore
Roll up a 30-inch length of No. 12 electrical wire and carry in a pocket of your hunting coat. If a shell jams in the chamber, unroll the wire, slide it down the barrel, and gently tap out. Also good for clearing obstructions from the barrel. Leave on the plastic insulation to prevent damage to the bore.

Muff Makes a Handy Hunting "Holster"
A fleece hand muff, worn diagonally across your stomach, makes a warm winter holster for a hunting handgun. Sew zippers on each end and the gun won't fall out. Add a disposable hand warmer and it will keep your hands warm, too. Comfortable, easy to get at, and the handgun stays well protected.

Listen to Your Dog
When pursuing game, never command a dog to go out onto ice or into a den when the dog is clearly reluctant to do so. In the excitement of the chase, a man may lose his best judgment before a dog loses its survival instincts.

Steel Shot Garbage Disposal Caution
When cleaning waterfowl, be sure to place the birds in the side of the kitchen sink without the garbage disposal. Unlike softer lead, a steel pellet that drops down the drain can lock up a disposal.

Painter's Coveralls Make Good Snow Camo
White painter's coveralls work about as well as special snow

camo and cost a lot less.

Cornstarch Helps Keep Your Powder Dry

When hunting in damp weather with a muzzleloader, prior to repriming after the first shot, sprinkle a small amount of cornstarch in the priming pan or nipple area, wait 5 minutes, and then lightly brush away. The cornstarch absorbs moisture. Pick and prime as always, and you're ready for your next shot.

Baking Soda Bath Makes Wild Meat Less "Gamey"

To remove the "game" taste from meat, place in a bowl and cover with cool water. Sprinkle generously with baking soda and let set 30 minutes. Drain, rinse, and pat dry.

Spray Foam Quiets Tree Stands

To quiet a tree stand made of hollow tubular bars, just cap one end of each tube and then fill with the expanding spray foam sold for insulating around windows. Dramatically reduces the banging and clanging.

Use Vest Loops for More than Shells

Most hunting vests have literally dozens of elastic loops for shotshells. Instead of filling them with more ammo than is ever needed, use the extras for a butane lighter, Band-Aids, toilet paper folded in cellophane, etc.

Use a Slingshot to Disperse Scents

Fill a gelatin-type pill capsule with scent and use a slingshot to shoot it where you want it without also getting your own scent in the area. To shoot longer distances, add sand to the capsule before filling with scent. An eyedropper works great for filling the capsules without getting the scent all over your hands.

Climbing Tree Stand Doubles as Work Platform

A climbing tree stand makes a great work platform when installing fixed tree stands. Install the climbing pegs as you descend. Also works well for trimming or topping trees.

Wet the Nose for a Happy Hunting Dog

Keep your bird dog sharp in hot, dry weather with water poured from a canteen or goat skin. Let the dog drink and wet its nose throughout the hunt. This keeps the dog hydrated and also helps its nose pick up scents.

Recycle Socks into Scent Trailing Pads

When the toes or heels wear out in athletic tube socks, wash with your other deer hunting clothes to deodorize and then cut off the foot and stretch the elastic tube top over your hunting boots. Spray with deer scent before you enter the woods to leave a scent trail straight to your stand.

Perfectly Dull Practice Arrows

Dull the point and the cutting edges of old broadheads, sharpen the back edges, and use them for target practice. The blunted broadheads don't penetrate a target as deeply, and the sharp back edge makes it easier to pull back out. The small amount of metal removed doesn't seem to cause any change in arrow flight.

Tree Stand Cord Doubles as Scent Dispenser

To hoist gear up into my tree stand, I use a cord that winds onto a reel. Before going out, I unreel the cord into a plastic bag with hunting cover scent, seal it and let it sit overnight. After pulling up my gear I reel the scented cord back down, and the scent dispenses over a wide area. You could do the same with a rope.

Silicone Restores Shell-Holder Loops

When a buttstock shell holder's loops stretch out and get too loose, rub a little silicone in each pocket, let it dry, and they will work as good as new.

Double Duty Compass/Sling Holder

Pin a round-ball compass onto the shoulder of your hunting jacket and it will help prevent a rifle sling slipping off. If you ever need it, you will have a compass, too.

LED Key Chain Safety Light

Attach an LED micro key chain light to your hunting coat to alert other hunters who may be approaching in early morning darkness. The micro beam will pinpoint your exact position yet doesn't seem to spook game.

Rice Helps Prevent Gun Rust

To help prevent a stored gun rusting, place a tablespoon of rice (not instant) in a coffee filter, fold the filter over, staple shut, and then place in the case with the gun. Will absorb moisture from the air. A few grains of rice in the camp salt shaker keep the salt running freely, too.

Crow Feathers Make Decoys More Lifelike

Save the longer feathers from the crows you shoot and use black electrical tape to loosely fasten about a half-dozen to the back of each plastic crow decoy. Even a light breeze ruffles the feathers, creating a more lifelike look.

Old Dog Collar Makes a Great Coyote Dragger

An old dog collar around the neck makes a dead coyote much easier to drag back to the truck.

Hula Hoop Helps Wrap Stand Strap Around Tree

When putting up a tree stand or tying on a safety harness, it can be difficult to get the straps around a big tree trunk. To solve this cut a child's hula hoop, tape the strap to one end, and then slip the open hoop around the tree. Turn the hoop around the trunk, and it brings the strap back around within easy reach.

One-Man Deer Loading Ramp

A 3-foot-wide sheet of 3/4-inch plywood makes it easier to load a deer in the back of a pickup truck. Lean one end on the tailgate with the other end on the ground by the deer. Roll the deer up as far as possible then pick up the ground end of the board and slide board and deer into truck.

Direct Dog to Crippled Ducks

When a crippled duck dives, it usually swims to the nearest shoreline and hides in cover near the water's edge. Instead of directing your dog to search where the duck fell, wait a few minutes and then have the dog check the nearby shoreline cover. The dog is much more likely to find where the duck came out of the water and then scent track it down.

Ground the Reloader for No More Static Cling

Before reloading shells, screw or tie one end of an electrical wire to the loader and stake the other end in the ground. This grounds out the static electricity so powder and lead no longer stick where they're not supposed to stick.

Grade "A" Wild Meat

When packaging cut-up game birds and animals, I sort the pieces by quality and label the freezer bags A, B, or C. It doesn't bother me to eat a bird that has been shot up and may have some broken bones, etc. But when I want to serve friends and family, they get the "A" bags.

Make Bandit-Style Face Mask from old Camo

Instead of discarding worn-out camo shirts, use the material to make bandit-style camo face masks. Cut a square from the back, fold the square diagonally in half over a shoelace, and tie the resulting triangle around your face below your eyes. Tighten or loosen as needed to adjust fit.

Distract Deer with Remote-Controlled Caller

To prevent deer spotting you as you leave a stand in the evening, set a remote-controlled caller 100 yards or so back on the trail as you walk in. When you want to leave, play a coyote howling sound and it will scare the deer off without alerting them to you or your stand. Just pick up the caller on your way out.

Waxed and Ready Hunting Guns

Put car wax on the metal parts of rifles and shotguns. It keeps them from rusting, doesn't rub off, and after a day or two gives off no odor. One good coat and you're set for the season. If you use it on the wood, too, the slippery feeling disappears quickly.

Put Blaze Orange on the Blind, Too

When hunting in a camo ground blind during deer gun season, pin an inexpensive blaze orange stocking cap to the very top of the blind. A stationary cap won't spook the deer, and it alerts other hunters to your presence.

Painting Gun Sights for Sore Eyes

To make open sights easier to see and use, try painting the front post white and the back blades fluorescent orange. When you look down the top of the barrel, the painted sights will be easily seen, especially if the target is darker in color, like a deer.

Use Pop Bottles for Reloading Shot

For handling shot without spilling at the reloading bench, rinse out soda bottles, dry them in the sun, use a funnel to pour in the shot, and then put the caps back on.

Tiny Bottle Makes a Mighty Squirrel Call

One of those tiny, corked vanilla bottles makes a handy squirrel call. Fill it with water, and when you want to call squirrels, simply pull the wet cork and work it up and down on the side of the bottle to make a range of "squirrely" sounds.

Snap-Hook Handy on Tree Stand Hoist Rope

Attach a snap hook to the rope you use for raising a gun and other items into your tree stand. Sure is easier than repeatedly tying and untying rope with cold hands.

Real Tail Improves Deer Decoy

Cure the tail from a deer in boric acid and use a large-head nail to pin it to the rear of a deer decoy. Attach a string so you can move the tail to give it more life. Deer watch that swishing tail, and they don't see you pulling the string—or your bow.

Use Plastic Food Wrap to Cover Scope Lens

The plastic food wrap in your kitchen cupboard makes a good see-through cover for a scope lens. Cut it at least an inch wider than the lens itself, stretch tightly over top and hold in place with a rubber band. Rain and snow wipe right off, and if you ever need to, you can pull it off quickly with your fingers.

Gun Bore Light Works for Dog Ears, Too

To see in my dog's ears, I use a gun-bore light made of fiber optics and bent at 90 degrees. It fits on the end of a small flashlight, and the bend keeps the light out of the way, allowing an unobstructed view down a gun's bore (or inside a dog's ear).

Reflective Tape Makes Arrows Easier to Find

To make it easier to recover shot arrows, first wrap reflective tape around the shafts. Tape shines in a flashlight beam.

Wax Bullets for Handgun Target Practice

Primer-powered wax practice bullets for centerfire handguns can be made by driving the spent primer out of a fired cartridge. Use a rattail file or drill bit to slightly enlarge the flash hole and press in a new small primer. Now press the cartridge case mouth down through a 1/2-inch-thick block of paraffin wax. The primer alone will shoot the wax wad cutter-type projectile accurately to about 25 feet. Corrugated cardboard suffices as a back stop. (*I recommend magnum primers and room-temperature wax for this. And, most important, file a highly visible notch in the rim of each case. Cases with enlarged primer holes can be used for no other purpose. Loading such a case with a powder charge and bullet load could be disastrous. – Ed Hall, Gun Editor*)

Cut Green Light Lens Cover from Plastic Bottle

The green plastic from a 2-liter plastic soda bottle makes a flashlight lens cover that won't spook game at night. Use the original lens for the pattern, and cut out with scissors.

Retractable Dog Leash Tree Stand Hoist
Compact retractable dog leashes work great for hauling guns and other gear up into a tree stand.

Instant Dog-Watering Bowl
Before taking a dog hunting in hot weather, cut a 15-inch square of sheet plastic, fold it up and put it in your pocket. When the dog needs a drink, stomp a hole in the dirt with your heel, place the plastic in the hole, and pour in water from your canteen. The dog will lap it up.

Pruners Also Handy for Dressing Deer
Hand-size pruning shears are great for clearing the limbs around a tree stand and also can be used to sever the pelvis bone in a male deer to make it easier to remove the bladder. Works much better than trying to chop through bone with a hunting knife. Clean with disinfectant and sharpen the blades with a flat file.

Dinged Arrow Shaft Recycled as Cleaning Rod
A dented or slightly bent aluminum arrow shaft can be used to push cleaning patches through shotgun barrels. The bowstring nock even holds the patch in place.

Ash Restores Turkey Friction Call
If a turkey friction call needs fresh chalk but you don't have any, dab ash on the striking surface and it will sound as good as new.

Squirrel Whistle Call Also Coaxes in Predators
A squirrel whistle call works well as a curiosity call for coaxing in hung-up predators. The call is the size of a quarter and can be attached by a lanyard to a coat zipper, where it's always handy.

Make a Landing to Teach Retriever Where to Go
When training a dog to retrieve in water, find a small pond with long grass growing around it and tromp down just a small area at the edge. Throw the dummy from there. When the dog swims

back, it will swim right to the opening and you. After several retrieves with lots of praise, it will always return to you.

Mark Ramrod to Show Empty and Loaded
Fully insert the ramrod in the barrel of a muzzleloader and mark it where it meets the end of the barrel. Now load the gun, insert the ramrod, and mark where it hits the end of the muzzle. With the rod marked this way, you can quickly check to see if the gun is loaded by simply inserting the rod.

Cow Pie Cover Scent
For an effective and totally free cover scent, step in a cow pie. The strong, natural odor works as well if not better than anything you could buy.

Antibacterial Scent Cover
Before hunting deer, rub Neosporen® (or another bactericide ointment) in your armpit. It kills the odor-causing bacteria that deer smell so well.

Cartridge Case Bore Guide
To make a bore guide for cleaning a bolt-action or break-open rifle from the breech end, remove the primer from a spent cartridge of the same caliber and drill out the primer hole large enough for the cleaning rod to pass through. Slip the cleaning rod through cartridge, attach cleaning tip, and then insert into the chamber through the breech. Cartridge case fits securely in the chamber, keeping the cleaning rod centered in the bore.

Tool Belt Doubles as Gun Carrier
Use a belt-style tool pouch to help carry the weight of a shotgun or rifle in the field. The butt end rests in the pouch with hands holding the forend and the barrel safely pointed up. From there, you can quickly and easily shoulder the gun for a shot.

Air Rifle Pump Handle Doubles as Shooting Rest
After cocking a spring-piston air rifle, pull the pump handle back

down for use as a shooting rest.

Grocery Bags Keep Game Pouch Clean
To keep a game pouch clean, use those thin plastic grocery store bags. They weigh next to nothing and fold flat to take up very little space. Bag individual squirrels, rabbits and grouse before sliding them in the pouch; pheasant tail feathers may stick out, but the pouch will stay clean.

Rubbing Alcohol Preserves Squirrel Tails
To preserve a squirrel tail for display, soak it in rubbing alcohol overnight. But first split it partway down, pull out the bone, and then run a sharp wire through the rest of the tail to make sure nothing blocks the alcohol soaking all of the way to the tip.

Cotton Rope Makes Cheap .22 Patches
Fifty feet of 1/4-inch cotton rope can be cut into 1/2-inch pieces to provide all of the cleaning patches you may ever need for a .22 rifle. Soak in solvent, gun oil or whatever you use then stick in the bore and push through with cleaning rod.

Recycle Old Sock as a Bowhunting Sleeve Guard
Old knee socks can be recycled into sleeve covers for bowhunting. Cut the foot off just in front of the heel, roll back and whip stitch around the opening to prevent unraveling. If the stocking has a crew knit at the top, it will grip the arm better and not slip. Holds loose sleeve off the bowstring, doubles as an arm guard, and provides a little extra warmth.

Recycle Old Freezer as a Gun Safe
An old, upright locking deep freeze serves well as a gun locker. It's airtight and has a lot of storage space. Leave a shelf in the top for shells and handguns. I doubt a burglar would even take the time to break into an old deep freeze in the garage.

Use a Fan to Air Dry Guns
Bring a cold firearm into a house and water may condense on the

metal. Putting the gun in front of a fan helps reduce this, though you still need to wipe the gun down with a treated rag before putting it away in the gun cabinet.

Gumout® Cleans Reloading Dies, Too
When a reloading die gets gummed with lube, spray it with Carb & Choke Cleaner from Gumout then let air dry. To speed the drying, use the "air in a can" sold for blowing the dirt out of computer keyboards.

Cotton Swabs Ideal for Cleaning Small Bores
Cotton swabs (the kind used to clean inside ears) also make ideal cleaning swabs for small bore guns. I bought a box of 500 generics for $4 and then cut each in two with scissors to make 1,000 swabs. The shaft of tightly rolled paper fits nicely in the end of a .17 cleaning rod, and they also fit .22 bores.

Pick Up and Recycle Brass Cartridges
When you get done shooting at the range, ask if you can pick up the cartridges lying around and then take them to a scrap yard. Helps keep the range clean, and with the high price of salvaged brass, you might even pay for your next box of ammo.

Truck Window Doubles as Knife Hone
You can use the top of a truck or car window as a hone to keep a fine edge on a field skinning knife. Roll the window down halfway and then use the top edge like a steel.

Laundry Clean Foam Ear Plugs
If you use foam ear plugs at the range, button them up in a shirt pocket when you are done and toss the shirt in the laundry. When the shirt comes out of the drier, the plugs will be soft and clean.

Pine Fresh Hunting Clothes
To put natural scent in hunting clothes, store them with pine boughs. Cut a piece of hardware cloth just a little bigger around than a clean garbage can. Put fresh-cut pine boughs in the bottom

of the can, then the hardware cloth, then your hunting clothes on top, and close the lid. The scent will rise and saturate the clothing, but the pine sap won't.

Boiling Water Straightens Plastic Arrow Vanes
To straighten wrinkled arrow vanes, dip in boiling water for 5 to 10 seconds or until the vanes straighten out. They stay straight after they cool.

Disposable Vet Gloves Ideal for Field Dressing
Disposable shoulder-length veterinary gloves fold up to the size of a matchbook and are ideal for field dressing big game. When done, pull the gloves off by turning them inside out and no other cleanup may be needed. The gloves are sold inexpensively at farm supply stores.

Precise 12-Gauge Slug Gun Bore Sighting
To precisely bore-sight a 12-gauge slug gun, remove the primers from fired 12-gauge and 20-gauge shotshells. Chamber the 12-gauge shell and put the 20-gauge shell backwards in the muzzle end. Secure the scoped barrel in a vise or on sandbags. Now look through the barrel to line up the primer holes on the target, and use the scope adjustment knobs to center the cross hairs on the same point.

Elevated Bucket Releases Aromatic Apple Dripping
Where baiting to attract deer is legal, drill holes in the bottom of a 5-gallon bucket, fill halfway with apples, and hang in a tree. As the apples slowly rot, they drip and release a strong aroma that is very appealing to deer.

Toboggan Keeps Lay-Down Field Blind Dry
A plastic toboggan (the kind kids use to sled in the snow) can serve as a waterproof bottom for a lay-down field blind. The raised sides help keep out the mud. Also good for hauling the decoys and gear; slides over grass almost as well as snow.

Stackable Venison Freezer Packs
When packaging ground venison for the freezer, flatten out the 1-pound packs until they are only an inch or so thick. Will stack like bricks and also thaw much faster.

Plant Natural Camo at Permanent Blinds
Plant tiger grass or another tall perennial around a permanent ground blind to add natural cover that is back each fall.

Dog Training Scent Fools Wild Canines, Too
Soak cotton balls in the rabbit scent sold for training hunting dogs and place them just downwind of a predator calling stand. When a canine hears rabbit squeals, circles downwind and also smells rabbit, it seals the deal. Also works at trapping sets.

Split Washer Locks Down Arrowhead
To prevent an arrowhead working loose, put a split washer between it and the shaft. (Note: The washer adds some weight; so shoot it to check and then adjust sights if needed.)

Olive Oil on the Whetstone
Use heavy olive oil on your whetstone. It leaves little if any odor; and when you clean game with a sharpened knife, it won't contaminate the meat with a petroleum product.

Charcoal Plinking Targets
Charcoal briquettes make great plinking targets. Sighting small, dark objects is good practice; they explode when hit; and the remains quickly biodegrade.

Tinkle Bell for Bowhunting Deer
When bowhunting from a ground blind, hang a small "tinkle" bell about 40 yards upwind and run a string from the bell back to your blind. When a deer is in front of the blind and you would like to draw your bow undetected, the light melodic sound draws the deer's attention without sending it packing.

Patch Preserves Dominant Eye Night Vision

To preserve night vision while driving between calling stands, wear a patch (like a pirate's) over your dominant shooting eye. Let your buddy do the driving, and leave the patch on until you are walking out to the stand, away from any light. You won't have to wait for your eyes to adjust before you can see to shoot. The Army teaches this, and it works.

Stinky Limburger & Syrup Bear Bait

To bait bear, rub a block of Limburger cheese into a rough-bark tree, making a thick smear 12 inches wide all around the trunk. Pour cheap pancake syrup over the cheese. Bears will come from near and far to lick and chew on that.

Grocery Bags Plump Up Turkey Decoys

After numerous packings, hollow, soft-foam turkey decoys tend to remain folded, especially the tail and neck areas. To remedy this, stuff with the thin plastic bags grocery stores use.

Recycle Swing Set Frame for Hunting Blind

Old swing set A-frames make excellent frameworks for quick hunting blinds. Just cover with a camo tarp or scrap plywood. Then brush it in by leaning fallen tree limbs against the sides.

Backache Heat Wraps Also Good for Warmth

The large heat wraps sold to relieve lower back pain can also keep you warm on a deer stand by raising your core body temperature. Toss a couple in your survival kit, too.

Milkweed Wind Indicator

Pick a couple of ripe milkweed pods and put them in a bag in your hunting kit. Then, when you aren't sure where air currents may be carrying your scent, just release a couple of the little floaters and watch.

Cleanse Deer Carcass with Fire

To remove the small hairs that seem to always cling to a skinned deer, adjust a small propane torch to the orange flame and then sweep it over the carcass. Quickly singes off all the hairs without hurting the meat or taste.

Froze-In Beaver Makes a Long-Lasting Bait Station
To make a long-lasting bait station for calling predators, chop a hole in an iced-over waterway and place a beaver carcass halfway in the hole. After it freezes in, it isn't going anywhere.

Cedar Needles a Natural Cover Scent
Use cedar needles to naturally cover your human scent. Just pull and twist to release the pungent oil, and then rub on boots. Spread around a ground blind and crush underfoot.

Black Marker Turns Blaze Orange into Camo Pattern
Use a black marker to draw lines on a blaze orange hunter's cap, imitating small tree branches. Breaks up the shape, making it harder for deer to see.

Bicycle Strobe Light Makes Night Deer Recovery Easy
The small flashing strobe lights on bicycles are great for marking a downed deer late in the day. If you can't get it out and must return with help after dark, a flasher on the trail or at the carcass will be seen easily from hundreds of yards away, and it will blink all night with fresh batteries.

Aluminum Foil Keeps Toes Warm & Toasty
To keep feet warmer while sitting in a cold stand, wrap your boots in heavy-duty aluminum foil. It creates a thermal barrier that holds cold out and body heat in. Enough to cover two boots folds into a thin square that fits in a pocket. The more layers under the boot, the better.

Pencil Mark Deer Tree Rubs to Check for Reuse
When you see a deer rub on a tree, make a mark through the middle with a thick carpenter's pencil. If the line is rubbed out when you check again later, you know the scrape is active.

Vacuum Pack Hunting Clothes with Pine Needles

Store hunting clothes between seasons in vacuum-pack garment bags. Very compact, and if you add pine needles before sealing the bag, the clothes come out naturally scented.

Metal Tubing Turkey Decoy Stilts

To make turkey decoys stand taller in high grass, cut "stilts" whatever height you want from metal tubing. Pick a diameter that the decoy stake will slide into, and paint the tubing black.

Pocket Gun Cleaning Kit

A pocket kit for field cleaning gun barrels can be made out of fishing line, a lead split shot and cotton rag. Double the length of the gun barrel and add 1 foot. Tie a loop in the end of the line and crimp the split shot on the other end. Now cut a cotton rag patch and double it over until it will pass through the bore snugly but without jamming. Open the action, drop the end of the line with the split shot down and out the barrel, put the rag in the loop, douse with bore cleaner, and use the line to pull the rag through the barrel. Fits in a pocket, and won't scratch the bore.

Acorn Cap a Natural Squirrel Call

Red oak acorn caps make great squirrel calls. When you suspect a bushytail is hiding in the treetops, scratch a trunk with the acorn cap. The sound reverberates up the wood, and often as not, the curious squirrel will come out and take a look. It works; just be ready to take a quick shot.

Taxidermy Eyes Enhance Decoys

To make decoys more realistic, add glass taxidermy eyes. They're inexpensive, easy to install, and take the illusion to a new level of believability.

Use Kiddy Pool for Cleaner Deer Hauling

Put a kiddy pool in the back of the truck, SUV or in a car trunk to haul home a field-dressed deer without making a bloody mess. Set the pool on the ground, load the deer, and then put it in the vehicle. Spray clean with a garden hose after use.

Use Anti-Seize for Choke Tubes
Instead of applying grease to shotgun choke tube threads, use the anti-seize lubricant sold at auto parts stores. It works far better and will not dry out. The Permatex® brand works well.

Velcro® Removes Tiny Hairs from Game Meat
After cleaning wild game, wipe the meat with Velcro® to pick off the tiniest hairs.

Suck the Ice Out of Mouth Calls
When a mouth call ices up, turn it around, suck with a fair amount of force, and it should clear.

Write the Date on Ammo Boxes
When you buy ammunition, always write the month and year on the box. You will be able to keep batches separate and also prevent the new mixing with the old.

Inner Tube Pieces Make Tree Stands Deadly Quiet
When building a permanent tree stand, sandwich pieces of old car or truck inner tube between the tree and the lumber pieces to deaden sounds. Even when the wind blows, no squeaks.

50 Cents + 50 Cents = $1 Squirrel Call
To make a simple yet productive squirrel call, wrap your index finger and thumb around a 50-cent piece and strike this "drum head" rapidly with the milled edge of another 50-cent coin. With practice, you can imitate the squirrel barking that brings curious squirrels out into the open.

Recycle Pyrodex® Box as a Loading Block
An empty Pyrodex pellet box works well as a loading block on the reloading bench. The square cells in a .50 pellet box stand up .30-06 cases nicely, and the .45 size also works well.

Soap Solution for Preventing Fogged Lenses
Rub a dry soap bar or squirt a little liquid dish soap or shampoo on the lenses of shooting glasses or eyeglasses then wipe off for instant fog-proofing.

Foaming Black Powder Cleaning Solution
To clean a muzzleloader, first rinse the barrel with cold water, as it removes fouling better than hot. Follow up with equal parts hydrogen peroxide, Murphy's Oil Soap and rubbing alcohol on a barrel brush. A few rapid strokes create foam that acts as a debriding agent. After the barrel dries, apply a rust preventative.

Always Tamp Flintlock When Priming the Pan
When you prime the pan of a flintlock, tamp the opposite side with your palm. This makes a gap between powder and touchhole. Due to this gap, upon firing, a force of air will send lit powder into the touchhole, igniting the charge faster.

Scotch-Brite™ Scrubs Plastic from Slug Gun Bore
To clean the plastic fouling out of a slug gun, cut a strip of fine-grit Scotch-Brite scrubber, soak it with gun cleaner solvent, wrap around a bronze brush one size smaller than the barrel gauge, and swab away. Works great.

Bring a String for Squirrels
When squirrel hunting, bring 30 feet of string. When a squirrel keeps circling to the wrong side of the tree, tie the string to brush, walk around to the opposite side of the tree, and pull. Often as not, the squirrel circles again, this time presenting a shot.

Foam Insulation Silences Tree Stand Squeak
To quiet the squeaking and creaking of a wood platform stand, spray the places that rub together with spray foam insulation.

Pump-Up Sprayer Cleans Hanging Big Game
Bring a pump-up garden sprayer to hunt camp, and when a skinned deer or elk is cooling on the game pole, use it to quickly

wash hair, dirt and blood off the meat. Use a new sprayer to be sure there has never been anything in it but water.

Calling All Critters

If you are getting no response to a turkey diaphragm call, or maybe just want to try something different, press the call firmly against the roof of your mouth with your tongue and blow real hard. Makes the most anguished sound imaginable, and any nearby fox or coyote will just have to investigate.

Recycle Kitty Litter Jugs for Shotshells

The jugs that hold 20 pounds of kitty litter, the ones with handles and wide screw-on lids, make great storage containers for the shotshells you plan to reload. Each one can keep more than 200 empty hulls sorted and dust-free. The jugs are stackable, see-through, and can be labeled with a marker.

Bucket of Frozen Beaver Bait Station

To make a bait station, freeze a beaver carcass in a 5-gallon bucket of water. Even big coyotes have trouble dragging it off.

Drinking Straw Protects Muzzle During Bore Cleaning

To protect the muzzle when cleaning a rifle bore, insert the cleaning rod through a plastic drinking straw. Now screw a nylon or brass jag onto the rod, making sure the rod still passes through the straw. Apply Hoppe's No. 9 to a patch and put it over the jag. (Some other cleaners will dissolve a plastic straw, so test first if you prefer another product.) Insert the patch 1/2-inch into end of barrel. Slide straw up rod to meet back of patch. Push rod and straw 4 inches into the barrel. Now hold onto the straw and continue pushing the rod all the way through. Repeat until patch comes out clean, and then run a couple of dry patches before finishing with G96 or Break Free.

Make a Mock Deer Scrape with Real Scrape Dirt

Dig up an inch or so of soil from an active deer scrape and use it to make a mock scrape near your stand. It will be more effective than any scent you might buy, because it's the real thing.

Use Cleaning Rod to Safely Dry Fire Shotgun
To dry fire a shotgun without damaging the firing pin, assemble an aluminum cleaning rod without the handle and drop just the rod down the barrel, flat end first. Put the butt of the shotgun on the floor, point the barrel up, and pull the trigger. The rod absorbs the strike of the firing pin, jumping in the barrel.

Cover Gun Muzzle with Finger from Elastic Glove
To keep snow and rain out of a gun barrel, cut a finger from a disposable elastic glove and stretch it over the muzzle. You can shoot right through it. Stays in place yet is easy to remove and can be reused again and again.

Check Trail Camera Cards On Site
You may view the photos from a trail camera on site by pulling the SD card and putting it in a digital camera. You can even erase the shots you don't want to save.

Recycle Old Crutch as a Standing Shooting Rest
An old crutch makes a sturdy standing-position shooting stick, and most are height-adjustable. Turn upside down and rest the rifle on the rubber tip. It will be steadier with the wider arm support on the ground.

Color-Code Your Handloads
When working up different handloads in the same cartridge, color-code the primers with Sharpie markers to help avoid any mix-ups later.

Make Efficient Deer Feeder with PVC Pipe
To feed deer without much waste, cut a 6-foot length of 4-inch PVC pipe and use bungee cords to fasten it to a tree, pointing up and down with the bottom opening a few inches off the ground. After filling the pipe with feed, put the bucket over the top to keep out snow and rain. To get a bigger or smaller pile of feed,

simply move the pipe up or down.

Mason's Mud Box an Easy-Load Deer Sled
A mason's open-end mud box makes a great sled for hauling deer behind an ATV. Just slide in the carcass. No lifting needed.

Battery-Power Scent Dispenser for Deer Lures
A battery-powered heated air freshener can be used to waft deer lure through the woods. Just add lure instead of air freshener scent. Turn it on when you hunt or just leave it running at a permanent stand.

Sawzall Blade Makes a Handy Handsaw
Use duct tape to secure wood handles to a new or slightly used Sawzall blade to make a compact saw easily capable of splitting the pelvis bone of a deer. May also be used to trim shooting lanes. Should fit easily in a pack or coat pocket.

Newspaper Bag Contains Turkey Mess
After you shoot a turkey, slip one of those plastic tube bags the newspaper comes delivered in over its head and neck. Secure with a rubber band, and it will keep the mess contained.

Real Horns Make Deer Decoy More Believable
To make a buck deer decoy more believable, replace the fake-looking plastic antlers (usually much too large, anyway) with a set of the real thing. A small five- or six-point seems to work best. Cut off the antler below the burr, drill a hole into the base, and glue in a large nail (minus the head). Stick these on the decoy head.

Use Deer Grunt Tube to Disguise Cough
Use a grunt tube to disguise the sound when you have to cough on a deer stand. Instead of spooking a buck, you may call it in closer. Put the tube down inside your coat or shirt to muffle the sound. If you are coughing loudly, reverse the tube and cough in the opposite end.

Easy Homemade Turkey Fan Display

For an easy homemade turkey fan display, all you need is a coat hanger and clothespins. Spread the fan out and pin the outside feathers to either side of the hanger, salt the "meaty" part, and let it dry.

Stalk Squirrels in Scuba Boots

Neoprene scuba boots are great for stalking squirrels, much quieter than hunting boots, let you feel the ground, and they don't leave recognizable tracks for others to follow. Might not be good everywhere, but a pair only costs about $20.

Trigger Block Gun Safety

Drill and tap a small hole through a gun's trigger guard behind the trigger and turn in a bolt until it is up tight against the trigger. The gun can't be fired or even dry-fired. When you want to shoot the gun again, simply back out the bolt.

Recycle Squeaker from Dog Toy as Predator Coaxer

Next time your dog shreds a squeaky toy, salvage that squeaker. Makes a great hands-free "coaxer" call for close-up predators. Inhale or exhale to get two distinctly different tones.

Tire Valve Stem Cap Keeps Your Powder Dry

A tire valve cap fits snugly over the nipple of many muzzleloaders, helping to keep the percussion cap and powder dry.

Recycle Dog Food Bag into Game Bag

Fifty-pound dog food bags are ideal for packing out elk quarters—tough and blood-proof. They weigh almost nothing and rolled up take little room in a pack. Put over the muslin game sack. Take off as soon as you are back at camp so air can cool the meat. Wash and reuse.

Toothpaste Cleans Gun Without Removing Blueing

To remove stains and light rust from fine gun metal, spread a little toothpaste on the affected spot and rub vigorously with a clean cloth. The Tom's of Maine brand does a great job of polishing gun metal without harming the blued finish.

Vegetable Brush Gives Game Hairs the Brush-Off
A stiff vegetable brush works great for removing the little hairs that cling to the meat after you skin a squirrel. Brush under cold running water for best results.

Band-aid Makes a Removable Scent Pad
To avoid contaminating clothing with cover or trailing scent, stick a Band-aid on a boot and add a drop to just the pad. Peel off to remove the scent.

One-Man Heated Hunting Stand
A one-man heated stand can be made from a 4-by-8-foot sheet of canvas, a can of cooking Sterno, and a hunting stool. Sit on the stool and wrap the canvas around your shoulders, overlapping over your legs. Place the lit Sterno at your feet. A can should keep you warm 3 or 4 hours on the coldest day. I've watched deer pass directly downwind without reacting.

Dry Sand Reduces Slipping in Icy Tree Stand
Keep a coffee can of dry sand at your permanent tree stand and sprinkle some on an icy floor to keep from slipping.

Tic Tac .22 Carrier
Carry a dozen .22 shells in an empty Tic Tac container. The little plastic box fits comfortably in a pocket; the lid snaps shut, and when you pop it open, rounds shake out one at a time.

Crow Call Ring Tone Won't Spook Game
Use a crow call for your phone ring tone and a call will not spook nearby game. A free app with great sound can be downloaded at the Play Store.

Bring Your Own Higher Ground for Scouting
Carry a section of aluminum ladder in the pickup truck when

heading out to look for game in the flats. Lean against a tree or the cab of the truck to get higher and glass a larger area.

Carpenter's Chalk-Line Reel Tree Stand Hoist
A carpenter's chalk-line reel makes a handy hoist for hauling gear up into a tree stand. Replace the cotton string with a nylon cord to make it stronger.

Grip Gloves Great for Pulling Arrows
A gardening glove or canvas work glove with rubber grip material on the palm helps when pulling arrows out of targets. Also helps grip the shafts when adjusting nocks, tightening broadheads, etc.

Recycle Belt into a Rifle Sling
Make a rifle sling from an old leather belt by simply trimming the ends to fit the swivels, folding over and punching a hole through. For a fastener, use a No. 12 button-head bolt, 3/4-inch long. Washers beneath the bolt head and the nut secure the joint, and a dash of JB Weld on the threads before tightening makes it even more secure.

Around-the-Neck .22 Shell Carrier
Cut a piece of leather from an old belt or shoe tongue. Pinch five holes in which .22 shells fit snugly. Tie it around your neck and you will be able to reload quickly without fumbling for a shell in a pocket.

Quarter Makes Muzzleloader Ramrod Easier to Use
When seating a charge with a muzzleloader ramrod, place a quarter on the end of the rod, your palm on the quarter, and then push. You will be able to apply more pressure with no pain.

Recycle Old Socks to Make Scent Trails
To leave scent trails, cut the top 2 inches of elastic cuff off a pair of old socks and slip them around the arches of your hunting boots. Apply scent before walking in to your stand.

Dental Floss Ideal for Sewing Bullet Holes in Pelts

Waxed dental floss is ideal for sewing up bullet holes and tears in pelts. It will not slip, is cheap and durable.

PVC Pipe Crow Decoy Stands

To elevate crow decoys, cut 3/4-inch PVC pipe into 5-foot sections and glue a connecting collar onto one end of the section. In the field, you can quickly join as many as is needed to reach any reasonable height. The stake on most crow decoys fits in the end of the pipe. A carry case can be made by cutting a section of 4-inch PVC drain pipe slightly longer than the 5-foot sections. Glue a cap on one end and slide another cap on the other end for a lid. For easier removal, drill a 1/8-inch hole in the middle of lid cap to allow air to enter as the cap is pulled off. Clamp a metal barn door handle to the middle for easy carry.

Shotgun Pellet Removal Tool

To make a tool for removing shotgun pellets before cooking game meat, hammer the point of a nail flat and slightly curved to form a miniature sharp-edged spoon. Insert this into each pellet hole, locate the pellet, and pop it out.

Compact Field Gun Cleaning Kit

For a handy field gun-cleaning kit, get an M16-style sectioned gun cleaning rod and cut a 3/4-inch PVC pipe to the corresponding length. Put rod sections, patches, etc. in the pipe, slide a cap onto each end, and you have a neat package only 8-1/2 inches long.

BB Target Trap from a Shoebox

Cut a piece of plywood to fit and then glue it inside the bottom of a shoebox. Put a target on the lid of the box, place crumpled newspaper in the box and then the lid back on the box, and you have a target that catches BBs, which may then be retrieved and fired again.

Steady Handgun Hold with a Lanyard

To hold a handgun steady, make a lanyard from a 6-foot length of 1/4-inch rawhide. Tie the ends together to make a big loop. At the opposite end of this knot, make a single overhand knot just large enough to fit the gun's grip. Place the big loop around your neck and slip the smaller loop around the gun's grip. Now hold the gun with a two-hand grip and extend both arms to pull the strap taut.

Really Keep Your Powder Dry

To waterproof a percussion muzzleloader cap, use windshield washer tubing, sold at auto parts stores for about 50 cents a foot. Cut into pieces about the same length as a percussion cap, and after the firearm is capped, slip one over the cap to seal out moisture and also secure the cap on the nipple. For added protection, place a tire valve stem cap over the tubing and nipple Pulls right off.

Camo Flap Makes a Better Hunting Cap

Cut a 1-foot square of camo cloth and stitch one edge around the back of your hunting cap. Cut out two large eyeholes. The hanging cloth helps protect neck and ears from sunburn, wind and insects. When hunting wary game like deer or coyotes, turn the cap around (bill in back, cloth in front) and you have a camo face mask. Just tuck the cloth inside the crown when wearing the hat around town.

PVC Pipe Muzzleloader Barrel Soaker

To soak a muzzleloader barrel in hot soapy water, cut a right-sized length of 4-inch PVC pipe and glue a cap on one end. Set the gun barrel in the pipe and then pour in the water. Afterwards, the PVC comes clean with warm water.

Wet or Dry Goose Decoys

Floating goose decoys cost more than field shells, so I turn the shells into floaters. At the local building supply store, I buy sheets of exterior house insulation, the type that goes in walls before the siding. It's 1-inch thick and comes in various colors. I set a shell decoy on the insulation, trace around the bottom, and cut it out with a utility knife. Now I slip it up into the decoy, leaving it flush with the bottom, and push four finishing nails through the plastic decoy and into the insulation. Finally, I wire a foot-long piece of 1/2-inch rebar rod to the underside like a keel, to add stability.

PVC Gun Cleaning Rod Holders
To store gun cleaning rods neatly out of the way, cut 1-1/2-inch PVC pipe to the desired lengths and use conduit strap and screws to attach to a ceiling or wall.

Chain-Style Camp Saw Doubles as Bone Saw
Use a flexible camp saw to cut through the big bones when field dressing deer and other big game. Add 5-inch wood dowel rods to each end to make handles that are easy to pass under a pelvic bone. Then you can just saw up and through.

Trash Bag Crow Decoys
Surprisingly effective crow decoys can be made by cutting heavy-duty black trash bags into 15-inch squares, wadding old newspaper into softball-size balls, placing a ball in each trash bag square, spinning it closed and then wrapping with electrical tape to hold it closed. Add a rock for windy days, and toss out in front of your field blind.

Palm a Quarter for Ramrod Comfort
When seating a charge and bullet in a muzzleloader, place a quarter on the end of the ramrod, your palm on top of the quarter, and then apply the needed pressure to send it fully home. This will save you from sore palms and errant shots caused by inadequate charge-seating pressure.

Trapping & Fur Handling

Mirror Handy for Checking Culverts

Culverts, burrows and other hidey holes can be great places to set traps, but leaning over to peer inside of one can lead to a nasty surprise, like getting sprayed in the face by a skunk. When a catch is made, the critter almost always tries to hide in the culvert, and you never know what might be in that trap. To avoid surprises either time, attach a bicycle mirror at an angle on a long handle, and use it to safely peer into the culvert from above.

Fleshing Beaver Without the Beam

I only trap about a dozen beavers each winter and have no other need for a regular fleshing beam. Instead, I lay a 3-foot-long 2-by-6 board on the bench. After skinning the beaver, I place just the outer edge of the pelt on this board and flesh the outer 2 inches with a small fleshing tool. After working all the way around, I stitch the pelt onto a hoop (properly adjusted for size) with 30-pound-test monofilament. After pulling it tight, I then flesh the remainder of the pelt flat on the bench. After wiping clean, the pelt is ready to hang and dry.

Jumper Cable Skinning Gambrel

To skin small furbearers, I suspended an old battery jumper cable from a rafter in my fur shed. The strong clamp holds mink and muskrat with no slipping. I also use it for raccoon and fox, but it works best with the smaller animals.

Use Shop Vac to Clean Critters Before Skinning

Use a wet/dry shop vac to draw the water and mud out of the fur before skinning and fleshing the critter. Use the upholstery-cleaner end to increase the suction.

Catfish Dough Bait Good for Trapping, Too

Catfish dough and stink baits make cheap and effective bait for trapping, too. Everything from weasels to raccoons to foxes will work the chicken blood or cheese variety, and it stays strong-smelling even in the coldest winter weather.

Lay Fox Belly-Up to Prevent Fur Slippage

After trapping (or shooting) a fox in the fall, always lay it on its back until you are ready to skin it. You may notice fur slippage if you leave a fox on its belly when the weather's warm. I believe the gastric acid escapes from the dead animal's stomach, and that makes the fur slip.

Window Weights on the Water 'Line

When trapping raccoons with waterline sets, attach old cast-iron window weights (may be salvaged from older homes) to the chains by the traps. When a coon is caught and pulls the trap from the bed, the weight may pull it down into deeper water to drown or at the very least prevent it pulling the foot up out of the water and chewing on it.

Cuts Improve Wood Stake Holding Power
When using a wooden stake at a water set, make four or five deep "rimming" cuts in the shaft of the stake, angled the same as the pointed end. You can easily push it into a mucky bottom, yet it will be twice as hard for an animal to pull back out.

Wax Boards for Easier Pelt Removal
Prepare wooden pelt stretching boards by rubbing them lightly with paraffin or candle wax. Pelts easily slide on and off, and it keeps the boards cleaner, too.

Make a Magnum Dirt Sifter
A big dirt sifter can be made from a 5-gallon plastic bucket and galvanized window screen. Place the bucket on the screen and trace around the bottom with a pen. Cut out the screen, making sure it is no larger than the inside of the bucket's bottom. Now cut out the bottom of the bucket, leaving a 1/2-inch shelf around the edge. Place the screen inside the bucket on this shelf, then hold it in place while using a propane torch to melt the metal screen into the plastic. Let cool and cut off the top of the bucket, leaving about 4 inches above the screen.

Recycle Rubber Waders into Fleshing Aprons
Waders usually wear out from the knees down. Instead of trashing them, cut them off above the knee to make a step-in fleshing apron. If you don't like the full backside coverage, it can be cut and strapped however you like.

Lay a Shower Curtain on the Fur Shed Floor
An old shower curtain on the floor makes for easy cleanup after skinning and fleshing. Because it is thicker it lasts longer and

handles better than most sheet plastic. Just take it outside, hose it off, and hang to drip dry.

Recycle a Mop into a Trapper's Wading Staff/Hook

Make a trapper's wading staff/hook from a worn-out mop's handle. Cut off one of the iron rods that hold the mop head in place; straighten out the other rod and bend into hook shape.

Windshield Scraper Works for Muskrats, Too

To scrape a muskrat, place the pelt on a wooden stretcher, place the butt of the stretcher in your lap, and scrape towards you with one of those plastic, handheld windshield scrapers. First sandpaper any sharp corners until they are round and smooth, and do not scrape any harder than necessary.

Air Compressor Pumps Up the Pelts

Get an air nozzle or air gun with a needle adaptor for your air compressor, and the next time you have a raccoon to skin, insert the needle nose in the animal's foot by the pad. Pump air in between the hide and the carcass until it looks like a football, and it will be much easier to skin.

Disposable Cardboard Floor for the Fur Shed

Large cardboard appliance boxes can be cut up to cover the floor of your fur shed. Duct tape the seams, and the cardboard provides a stable surface that soaks up the grease, etc. Also cushions tired feet. When the cardboard deteriorates, or at the end of the season, simply discard.

Stretch Shellfish Oil with Corn or Vegetable Oil

To make costly shellfish oil scents go further, try mixing it with corn oil or vegetable oil. Both smell like what coons naturally like, and even diluted shellfish oil emits a strong scent.

Weak Traps Best for Teaching Beginners

I used an old No. 1 with next to no spring-power left to teach my young son how to set a trap. He loved setting it, and it never once hurt his fingers.

Case-Skin Beaver for Easier Fleshing

For easier fleshing, case-skin beavers. You will be able to maintain better control on the fleshing beam than if it was skinned open with a cut up the middle. After you are done fleshing then cut up the middle and tack down to dry.

Make Weasel & Squirrel Stretchers from Coat Hangers

Cut the shoulder ends off of wire coat hangers to make weasel and squirrel stretchers. Bend the ends to spring apart a little, and can pin the legs with clothespins.

Nice Shades, Trapper

When water trapping, wear a pair of polarized sunglasses. You may be amazed by how much easier it is to see muskrat and beaver den entrances, runs, and other underwater objects.

Use Lettuce Plants to Cage-Trap Groundhogs

For groundhog cage bait, pick up a small flat of lettuce plants. Remove a plant, wrap plastic loosely around the roots and secure with a twist tie. Soak the plant with water from a spray bottle and place it in the cage. Spray again when checking traps, and it will stay fresh and green for days.

Store Cage Traps Between Floor Joists

Store 15-inch cage traps between the joists in a basement ceiling. The rafters are 16 inches on center, and the traps fit snugly and are easy to secure with hooks or wire.

Tail Zipper for Beaver, Too

Those "tail zipper" devices also can be used when skinning beavers to make the long, straight cut from the base of the tail to the hip across the belly.

Fresh Frozen Raccoons Easier to Flesh

After skinning a raccoon, roll the green hide in a ball, fur out, and put it in the freezer overnight. The next day, partially frozen fat just rolls off the hide, making it much easier to scrape clean.

Put the "Jump" Back in Underspring Traps

To revive underspring jump traps, weld a 6d nail under the spring where it meets the frame or just wrap with No. 6 bailing wire four or five times and twist-tie underneath the trap frame. This boosts the leverage, pumping life back into the spring.

Plant Lure Bottles and Waste Not, Want Not

Instead of throwing away empty bottles of trapping lure, push them into the ground up to the bottle neck at trap sets. The residue in the bottle will keep working for a long time. Empty bait jars can be used the same way as scent attractors in box traps.

Use Portable Drill to Make Rock Anchors On Site

While scouting streams for trapping, I carry a cordless drill with a 3/16-inch masonry bit. It is a simple matter to find a suitable rock and then drill a hole for attaching a drowner wire that will not slip off. Saves lugging a lot of weight around later.

Hog Rings Attach Beaver Pelts to Hoops

Hog rings work great for attaching beaver pelts to hoops. Use a pliers-type leather punch to make small holes 1/8-inch in from the edge of the pelt. This avoids accidentally poked fingers, and the clean cuts by the leather punch resist tearing. When the pelt dries, the holes look the same as if you had nailed the pelt.

Tangle-Free Trapping with Recycled Grocery Bags

To prevent tangling, place each trap, chain and grapple in one of those super thin but tough bags they use at the grocery store. Works great, adds no bulk or weight, and costs nothing.

Taint Bait without the Odor or Mess

When allowing a quart jar of chunk bait to "ripen," I stretch a latex skinning glove over the mouth of the jar. The glove inflates to contain the gas that forms as the meat taints, with no smell getting out and no bugs getting in.

Recycle Squeeze Bottles for Trapping Lure
The squeeze condiment bottle, such as mustard comes in, may be cleaned and then used to carry and dispense trapping lure or urine. It may be necessary to thin lure with glycerin, which also acts as an antifreeze.

Mop Bucket Does Double Duty on Trapline
Two-compartment mop buckets are great for carrying gear and supplies on a trapline. Put traps and stuff that you want to keep scent-free in one side. Lure, bait and the like go in the other.

Toothpicks Make Subtle Trapping Scent Holders
Put 10 to 15 round toothpicks in a 1-ounce bottle of lure. When you need a scent stick to push into the ground at a set, you will have one at hand with plenty of scent already absorbed. It's convenient, and you waste none of the valuable lure.

Handy Bag-o-Bait for Trapping
Crawdads and small fish make excellent bait for raccoons and mink. Seine all you want during summer and freeze in small, resealable plastic bags, six to the bag. Thaw and carry just what you need each day, with no mess and little odor.

Prevent Bandits Stealing Cage Bait
To stop raccoons reaching through cage traps to steal the bait, cut sections of smaller wire mesh (small enough that a raccoon's paw can't get through) and attach to the sides and back of the cage where you place the bait.

Minnow Traps Also Catch Mice
Funnel-type minnow traps also catch rodent baits for canine trapping. Bait with dog food and cover lightly with hay. Mice and voles easily enter, but same as the minnows, can't seem to find their way back out.

Bring Longsprings Back to Life

To restore a weak spring in an old longspring trap, put the spring in a table vise in such a way that closing the vise pushes the bend apart. Works great and costs nothing.

Fork Makes a Great Burr Puller

To remove a burr before fleshing a pelt, wet the fur with soapy water, slip an ordinary table fork under the burr and pull it out. Heavy stainless steel forks work best. I have used currycombs and other methods, but this works best by far.

Recycle Birdhouse Nests as Attractors at Sets

We clean a number of birdhouses in the fall right before trapping season and then use the nests and other smelly contents as attractors at flat sets for fox and raccoons.

Duct Tape Spool to Keep Wire Tangle Free

To keep a spool of 16-gauge trapping wire from unrolling, wrap a couple of layers of duct tape around the outside edges of the spool. Now pull the wire out from the center opening.

Leave Trapping Bait on the Cob

Cut an ear of field corn crossways into five or six sections. Punch a small hole through the center of each piece and insert the stem and top from a dried goldenrod, about 8 inches long. Pushed into the bank above a trap set just underwater, these make quick coon and muskrat sets.

Pinpoint Trap Placement with Needle-Nose Pliers

Use needle-nose pliers to lower set leghold traps underwater. Makes it easy to bed the trap exactly where you want it without accidentally setting it off.

Restore Trap Levers with Small Washers

When the spring pin holes in coilspring trap levers become oversized and oblong due to use, braze small washers to the outsides of the levers. Be sure to use the proper size washer to match the spring pin.

Use Snow to Dry-Clean Fur
Briskly rub snow into the fur after an animal has been removed from a trap to clean and dry the fur very effectively.

Deep-Fried Trap Preparation
When I need to clean and dye just a few traps during fox season, I do it with an old double-deep fryer bought at a garage sale. With cleaning solution in one side and boiling black walnut hulls in the other, I can clean and dye a few traps in short order. Never leave a heating deep fryer unattended. They come to a hard boil very quickly.

Cock the Springs to Let Longspring Jaws Set Flat

Side view shows spring raising jaw.   *Twist springs to level jaw.*

Spring tension will raise the loose jaw on a double longspring trap. To let it set flat, twist the springs a little bit back towards the other jaw. The trap will now lay as flat as any coilspring.

Drain Holes Keep Bucket Upright in the Water
Drill plenty of 1/4-inch holes in the bottom and lower sides of the 5-gallon plastic bucket you use to carry equipment on the water line. When you set the pail down in the water, the holes allow water in, which keeps the bucket from tipping. The bucket drains almost instantly when you pick it back up.

Old Pie Pan Makes a Lightweight Dirt Sifter
To quickly make a lightweight dirt sifter, simply drill enough holes in an old aluminum pie pan.

Carryout Coon Bait

Those small jelly packets in restaurants may be bought in quantity at a restaurant supply, and peeling back the wrapper about a third of the way to expose the jelly makes for a neat little trapline sweet bait. Use a paper punch to put a small hole in the rim of the container so you can hang it. A container spinning on the breeze should pull in a raccoon for a closer look. Grape works well, along with a little commercial coon lure. (First check the restrictions on visible bait to make sure you can do this legally where you trap.)

Lye Solution Good for Cleaning More than Just Traps

When you are done boiling traps, use the remaining lye solution to clean the rust from garden tools, log chains, etc.

Trapper's Staff/Hook from Old Hoe

To make a sturdy trapper's staff/hook, hacksaw the blade off an old hoe leaving the metal hook part still attached to the shaft.

DIY Trap Capper from an Aerosol Can Cap

Make a "trapper's cap" with a 3/4-inch wooden dowel and the cap from an aerosol can. Cut the dowel to length and attach the cap with a small screw and washer. Cut a notch for the trap pan dog, and you are done. Place cap over the trap pan and you can pack dirt around the jaws without getting any under the pan.

Fillet Knife for Furbearers

An old fillet knife works great for skinning raccoons. The sharp part of the blade down by the handle "rings" the back legs and cuts around the neck behind the skull with ease. Cut the tail right next to the hip, and it, too, comes off with ease. Then use the sharp point to slit the hide up the back legs to the rectum.

Recycle Old Waders into a Waterproof Pants Seat

When leaky old hip waders can no longer be patched, cut off at the knees and the tops can be slipped on over pants to keep your bottom dry when making ice sets or sitting on wet ground.

Recycle Backpack into 5-Gallon Pack Basket

When a school backpack wears out, take the back straps off and bolt them onto a 5-gallon plastic bucket, with two bolts on each strap in case one lets go. Also attach the pouches from the bag on the inside of the bucket to hold pliers, lures, etc.

Prevent Kick Back with Stick in Springs

The springs on double longspring traps may be twisted towards the dog after setting so the trap's loose jaw will set level. But spring tension may make the springs twist back the way they were, causing the free jaw to rise again. This is easily fixed by inserting a short, stout stick through the springs. The stick braces against the crosspiece just below the dog and is held there by the tension of the springs. With a single-spring trap, the stick goes through the spring, under the pan, and rests on the left side of the end of the base of the trap. Always use dry, seasoned sticks where there are beavers, because beavers will chew a freshly cut green stick.

Stick holds springs so they can't kick back.

Traffic Cone Fleshing Beam

Traffic cones make great little fleshing beams. Just clamp or nail to a workbench, slip a skin over top, and go to it. They come in different sizes and are discarded by utility companies once they fade or get too dirty.

Make Swinging Cage Trap Bait with Marshmallows

Thread a half-dozen marshmallows onto an 8-inch length of 17-gauge wire. Fold the end of the wire over a cotton ball to keep the marshmallows on the wire. Make a hook out of the other end of the wire, dip the cotton ball in a liquid bait or lure, and then hang the hook end to the inside top of a cage trap, behind the treadle pan. When the wind blows, it swings, adding sight appeal to the scent spreading over the area.

Raccoon Fat Preserves Stretcher Boards

I use a cotton cloth to wipe coon hides as they dry. At the end of the season, I use this oily cloth to wipe mink boards before putting them away. The boards last longer, and next season, pelts are easier to remove.

Beaver Meat Just Too Tasty to Waste

Instead of throwing away beaver carcasses, I grind the best back straps and hind quarters into burger for my own table. The rest goes to local hunting dog owners who gladly accept the high-protein meat.

Use Baby Food Jars to Taint Single-Set Baits

Put fish parts in a little baby food jar, set it in the sun until it stinks and then bury it. Come trapping season, just place the bait where you want it, take off the lid—and run.

Cupcake Pan Covers

Cupcake pan liners make great pan covers for No. 1-1/2 coilsprings. Also put under the trap to help keep the jaws from freezing down. They are inexpensive and come cut to size, lightly waxed and ready to use.

Tent Stakes Double as 110 Bodygrip Holders

Tent stakes are excellent for supporting smaller bodygrips. The prong that protrudes from the stake slips over the main spring to hold it upright. Also put the stake through the ring of the chain.

Put Clear Tape Over Lure Bottle Labels

Before trapping season, cover the labels on lure bottles with clear Mylar tape; this keeps the labels readable through mud and water. Attach trapline pliers to the top of your backpack with 14 inches of chain—saves much time looking for pliers, and you cannot leave them behind. Use a staple gun to tack hides to wooden stretchers. The taller 3/8-inch staples leave more room for easier removal.

Recycle Waders as Trapline Pants Protectors
Cut the boot parts off of leaky old hip waders. Before hiking in wet weeds, slip on over your jeans to keep pants dry. Also makes a good scent barrier, allowing you to forgo a kneeling cloth while making sets.

Fiberglass Assures Trap Pan Will Drop
Cut a piece of spun fiberglass insulation the size of the trap pan and place it under the pan. It's lightweight, scent-free and keeps dirt out, allowing the pan to drop freely.

Trapper Orange a Good Idea, Too
During deer gun season, we spray paint our 5-gallon buckets hunter orange just to be safe.

Ask a Taxidermist for Trapping Bait
A busy taxidermist may provide lots of free trapping bait. The last time I checked, I left with a 5-gallon bucket of skinned walleye and lake trout.

Trap Jaw Laminations Need to Be Squeaky Clean
Traps with laminated jaws need to be cleaned thoroughly between the jaw and the added lamination strip. Hair, blood, etc. gets embedded in this tight area, and if not removed may be detected by a sharp-nosed fox or coyote.

Plywood in the Bottom Saves Pack Basket
Before using a new pack basket, cut a piece of 1/2-inch plywood to fit and place it in the bottom of the basket. Saves the webbing and greatly increases the life of the pack basket.

Nose Hangers for Thawing Green Pelts
When the fur is coming in heavy, I freeze green pelts to be processed later. Before freezing, I tie a 6-inch length of 16-gauge wire through a nostril hole and form the other end into a loop.

I roll pelts fur side out from tail to head with the wire loops sticking out the ends and pack two or three in a bag. When I remove them from the freezer, I hang them by the nose wires to thaw. They unroll on their own and shed moisture, too.

Lucky Horseshoe Trap Grapples
Make grapples for fox trapping by welding pairs of horseshoes to 15-inch pieces of rebar.

Bumper Jack Trap Puller
Weld a short length of 3/8-inch chain with a hook on the end to the lift portion of an old bumper jack and it works very well for pulling stubborn trap stakes. Weld the plate to the bottom with the handle and the jack doesn't fall apart.

Throw-Away Cardboard Fur Stretchers
Make throw-away fur stretchers from heavy cardboard appliance boxes. Simply cut out two pieces the size and shape you need and glue them together. One box will yield quite a few coon stretchers, and when they start to wear around the edges, cut them down to mink or muskrat size. Most appliance stores gladly give away the boxes.

Duct Tape Stretcher Boards for Easier Pelt Pulling
Coon pelts can be hard to pull off stretcher boards (especially plywood). To fix this, run 2-inch-wide duct tape from the top to the bottom along both edges of the board, wrapped with about 1 inch of tape on each side; pelts will be much easier to pull off.

Recycle Corduroy Pants as Pelt Wipers
Use material cut from old corduroy pants legs to remove the globs of fat left behind after a pelt has been fleshed. Fat sticks like glue to corduroy.

Collect Trapping Dirt at River Boat Launches
To quickly collect large quantities of dirt for bedding traps, go to a boat access ramp on a river in the spring right after the

high water has gone down and shovel the accumulated silt into 5-gallon buckets. It must be sifted, as there will be a good deal of debris mixed in, but after sifting and drying, the fine, sandy material is perfect for bedding traps.

Pipe Makes a Handy Stake-Dipping Tool

To treat steel trap stakes with speed dip, cut a piece of 2-inch pipe 26 inches long (longer for stakes over 24 inches, wider if you have oversized nuts and washers welded on the ends of the stakes). Solder a cap on one end and bury that end of the pipe in the ground. Now, simply fill the pipe two-thirds with speed dip and lower a stake into the pipe to coat one end. Take out, let dry, and then dip the other end. No waste, and no mess.

Cover Traps with Campfire Ashes

Pass clean wood ashes through a dirt sifter into plastic bags and tape shut. After making a dirt set, sprinkle these ashes over the ground on top of the bedded trap. Ashes attract coon and fox while also helping to cover any human scent left at the set.

Finders Keepers with Surveyor Flagging on Drag

Attach 6 feet of bright orange surveyor's flagging to a trap drag before burying it at a set. It will be much easier to find later, should a trapped animal drag it away.

Mark Traps in Code to ID Later

To permanently engrave traps as yours, don't use initials as these can be filed down or altered should someone else "find" the traps. Rather, drill a couple of very small holes inconspicuously through the frame or one of the jaws. The trap is permanently marked, and no one will be the wiser.

Vise Grips Great for Setting Double Longsprings

Vise grip pliers make it easy to set double longspring traps. Use the locking pliers to compress and hold one spring down while leaving both hands free to compress the other spring and set the trap. The long-nose style works best.

Peat Moss Makes Great Trap Bedding

Peat moss sheds water and makes a great weather-resistant bedding for traps; 100-percent natural with no added scents.

Bite-Size Trapping Treats

Soak bite-size shredded wheat cereal in trapping lure and put in a wide-mouth jar. After making a dirthole set, drop one or two of these soaked cereals in the hole. Saves time and mess.

Check Deer Snare Stops with a Pop Can

Ohio law requires a deer stop to prevent a snare from closing to a diameter of less than 2-1/2 inches. To check this when putting on deer stops, tighten the snare loop around a regular pop can. It has a diameter of 2-1/2 inches. Most states have a similar size restriction, but check first.

Fish Fertilizer Doubles as Trapping Lure

If you run out of trapping lure during the season, try fish emulsion plant fertilizer. It works so well for coon and gray fox you may move it from the garden shed to the fur shed.

Back Cut Salvages Damaged Beaver

The large chewed areas on the backs of spring beavers can ruin them for the fur market. But for home use, skin them with a cut up the back instead of the belly. This puts the chewed fur at the edges and leaves the undamaged belly fur whole. The belly fur is almost as nice and makes wonderfully soft mittens, etc. Likewise, cutting from the back instead of the belly lets you harvest clean loin and thigh meat from gut-shot rabbits.

Bagging Snares and Cover Dirt

Put individual snares in small, resealable plastic bags and they do not tangle. Mark the outside of the bag to tell them apart. I mark mine with a "B" (for beaver), "F" (for fox), "R" (for raccoon), etc. Instead of hauling a bucket of dry dirt around, I fill a few of these same bags with enough dry dirt, buckwheat hulls or peat moss for a remake. One per set. No mess, and the bags are reusable.

Recycle Backpack Frame into Pack Basket
Make a trapping pack basket from an old square pack frame (the kind with a sleeping bag bar on the bottom) and a heavy-duty rubber storage box. The storage box rests on the bar and is secured to the frame with bungee cords, making it easily removable. Snap-on lid keeps snow and rain out and gear in.

Coon Bait on the Cob
Add chunks of dry corncob to a container of trapping bait. After the cob absorbs liquid and scent, it gives off scent better than the bait itself and can be pinned down at the set to decrease nuisance bait pilfering.

Fillet the Fat Off a Frozen Flat-Tail Pelt
To remove the bulk of the fat from a beaver hide, stretch it on a hoop then put it outdoors to freeze. Bring it in frozen and use a sharp knife to "fillet" off the heavy fat. When it thaws, you can finish scraping it with less mess and effort.

Dog Snap Trap Attachment
If you're a weekend trapper and must pull traps after a night or two, instead of using S-hooks, weld loops on the ends of the stakes and put dog snap "D" rings on the ends of the trap chains. This allows you to leave the stake in and pull the trap with no tools. Then, when you set the trap again next week, it only takes a second to snap it back on the stake. As a bonus, most snaps are made with a swivel.

Ice Pick Handy for Hooping Beaver Pelts
Hooping beaver pelts is easier when a sharp ice pick is used to poke the holes through the hide for the hog rings.

Lanolin Treatment for Home Tanning
When tanned hides are drying after the pickling stage, work lanolin hand cream into the leather a couple of times. The leather

will be softer and somewhat waterproof with a pleasant smell.

Vinegar Takes the Shine Off Metal
To take the shine off of new zinc-plated chain, cable, S-hooks, etc., place in a plastic pail and cover with white vinegar (5 percent acid). Within 6 hours, the plating is dissolved. Rinse the dulled metal in hot water and let it rust just enough to take dye. Save the vinegar for use on the next batch.

'Taint a Problem with Right Jar Lid
Taint meat baits in a quart canning jar with the lid on but the retaining band a little loose. Gases will escape yet flies won't get in. Leave jars in full sun until desired taint, usually three to four days, then add the fixative and move to a cool, dark place. Gallon size can be used to render fish oil.

Hemlock Lure Holder
Pick up hemlock cones, put them in a jar, and pour in some fox lure. Makes the lure go further as the cones hold the scent, and they look natural at sets.

Trap Set in a Bag
Once my land traps have been cleaned, dipped, and dried, I store each in a clean plastic bag along with enough dry sifted dirt to make a set. Speeds up set making, and the traps smell like the covering dirt with no contaminating odors.

Calling and Snaring Go Together
Set snares in the trails and fence crawl-unders around a field. Then, in the morning before checking them, call with a rabbit squealer. A fox or coyote responding to the call may be snared on the way in, and you may get a shot at one that misses the snares. Works best right at dawn; no need to overdo the calling.

Inner Tube a Water Line Workhorse
For water trapping, mount a piece of 1/2-inch plywood on top of a 15-inch inner tube and attach some bungee cords for holding

traps and other gear. An inner tube can easily carry 100 pounds yet floats freely in shallow water.

TP Bullet Hole Plug Keeps Pelt Clean
After dispatching a trapped animal, plug the bullet hole with toilet paper to stop the bleeding and keep the pelt clean.

Cover Trap Pans with Coffee Filters
Coffee filters make great trap pan covers. A pack of several hundred only costs a couple of bucks, and they come in the right shapes and sizes to fit most traps.

Handy Hook-Blade Tail Splitter
A disposable blade utility knife with a hook blade, the kind used to cut shingles, makes a great tail splitter. Also good for the opening cut on deer, beaver, etc. When the disposable blade dulls, just pop in a replacement.

Rust Neutralizer Saves Trap Steel, Too
To restore old traps, sand off the surface rust and then etch the metal with zinc phosphate rust neutralizer (available at auto restoration suppliers). A final light coat of boiled linseed oil seals the metal, preventing further corrosion.

Vegetable Oil Slides Burrs Out of Furs
To make burrs easier to remove from furbearers, use a pump or spray bottle to lightly apply cooking oil to the fur then comb out.

Cotter Pin Tail Stripper
A cotter pin in the 4-inch range splayed apart just enough to fit over the tail of a coon or fox, pressed tightly and pulled firmly, works great as a tail stripper.

Fill Muskrat Holes with Leaves to Check Use
When scouting muskrat locations, bring a trash bag of leaves and fill the bank and den holes. Muskrats will push out the leaves, and you will know which holes are active and worth setting.

Umbrella Rib Tail Skinner

The metal rib from an old umbrella makes a good tail skinner tool, pointed with a slot running the entire length. Push the rib, slot side up, as far as it will go up the tail between the skin and the tailbone. Then put knife tip in the slot and run it up the rib. Safely makes a very neat cut.

Flesh Beavers with an Electric Knife

To quickly flesh beavers with less effort, use an electric meat carving knife or a cordless electric fillet knife.

Collect Cat Scent from Litter Box

If your cat uses a litter box, fill it with Speedy Dry instead of a scented cat litter. When you dump the litter out, the urine will be stuck to the bottom of the box. Scrape it out with a putty knife and into a jar to be saved until trapping season. A teaspoon of this down the back of a dirthole gives off plenty of coyote-attracting odor.

Surplus Store Folding Shovel for the Trapline

A military surplus folding shovel is a great tool on the trapline. Compact for easy carry. Digs like any shovel, and in the 90-degree position, great for skimming ice, uncovering sets, etc.

Wintergreen Minty Fresh Skunk Odor Mask

The best masking agent for skunk odor is synthetic oil wintergreen (methyl salicylate).

Acrylic Spray Keeps Labels Readable

Spray clear acrylic over the labels on lure bottles and bait jars to keep them readable. It's faster and works better than clear tape.

Combo Dirt Carrier/Sifter

Save two of the plastic snap lids from 2-pound coffee cans and drill a close pattern of 1/4-inch holes in the bottom of one can to make a handy carrier/sifter for bedding dirt. With a lid on top and bottom, you can carry a full can from one set to the next.

Trap Thieves "Foiled" with Aluminum

I used yellow survey ribbon to mark trap sets, but due to trap theft, I switched to a small piece of aluminum foil wrapped tightly around a branch on a nearby bush. Thieves do not look for this the way they look for ribbon, and in the dark, it reflects a flashlight beam, making the set easy to find.

Leaf Blower Doubles as Fur Dryer

A leaf blower will quickly blow-dry wet furbearers for easier handling, and it puts a nice fluff on the fur.

Winter-Proof Trap Sets with Urea

We buy 50-pound bags of pelletized urea at the feed store to use as trap set antifreeze. We carry it on the line in dry 20-ounce water bottles. Just unscrew the bottle top and sprinkle as needed.

Reading a Rusty Old Trap Tag

If you find an old trap with a tag that is too rusty to read, rub the surface with coarse sandpaper. It gets shiny, but the stamped name and address remain dull because the sandpaper does not reach the stamped-in letters.

Vise Grip & Razor Blade for Skinning

Clamp a razor blade in a vise grip for an adjustable-angle skinning knife for beavers and other big animals. To change the angle, simply reposition. When it gets dull, put in a new blade.

Orange Trapline Tools Harder to Lose

Paint the handles of trowels and other trapping tools bright orange, followed by a coat of spray varnish. This will help you locate any misplaced tool in the shed or out in the woods. The varnish also helps the wood handle last longer.

Bacon Grease & Dog Food Raccoon Bait

For inexpensive raccoon bait, mix cheap dry dog food with dirty bacon grease. The scent attraction lingers for weeks.

Bicycle Pump Helps with Hide Removal

With a bicycle pump and a basketball needle, you can pump enough air under the hide of a muskrat, mink, or weasel to make it separate from the carcass for easier skinning. Cut a slit in the underside of a rear leg, insert a pencil and move from side to side. Pull the pencil, insert the needle, pinch tight and pump.

Cotton Ball Lure Holders

To save time and not waste trapping lure, dab a little on as many cotton balls as will fit in a tall pill bottle (use a separate bottle for each scent). When making a set, pull a scented cotton ball out with a stick and place it wherever you want it.

Auto Shammy Towels Dry Fur Fast

The super-absorbent synthetic "shammy" towels sold at auto supply places are also great for drying wet furbearers. When done, just rinse, ring out and hang to dry.

Recycle Snow Shovel Handle onto Trapping Trowel

Recycle the heavy-duty plastic D-handle from a worn-out snow shovel by sliding it over the straight wood handle on a trapping trowel. A few wraps of duct tape over a couple of wood screws should snug it up. Your wrists will thank you.

Beaver Castor Drives Fox Wild

If you have trouble with a shy fox digging at traps, drop a fresh beaver castor sac in the dirthole. The smell excites the fox so much it works the set with gusto.

Belly Up to the Fleshing Beam

For working furs on a fleshing beam, make pelt-holding pads that go around your waist by cutting scrap carpet 6 inches wide and 20 inches long. Use a hot awl to melt slots about 1 inch in from each end, and a short shock cord or bungee will hold it securely around your waist. Pinch a pelt between your padded belly and the beam, and it won't slip or slide.

Goose Wing Feather Duster for Trap Sets

The wing of a Canada goose works great as a brush to blend the covering at dirt sets—lightweight yet strong and stiff enough to move clods, small stones, etc.

Convert Trap Rust to Coating

"Rust converter" spray bonds right to the metal, so I tried it on lightly rusted traps and it worked great. Left a nice dark color, and the odor dissipated in a few days. Maybe not traditional, but quick and easy. A can costs about $4 and goes a long way.

Baster Handy for Handling Trapping Scents

When rendering down fish, meat, etc., for use as trapping scent, use a squeeze-bulb turkey baster to transfer juice from big jars to smaller bottles.

Butter Knife Helps Remove Hides Without Damage

When skinning furbearers, use a butter knife to work the hide off the carcass. It will slice through the fat and even cut thin membrane but not the hide.

Lure Skunks into Cage Traps with Buttered Popcorn

Butter-flavored popcorn is cheap to make and works great for luring skunks into cage traps.

Save Tuna Juice for Trapping Scent

When opening cans of tuna, instead of draining the juice down the sink, save it in a container in the freezer. Then, when trapping season rolls around, you will have plenty of "fishy" scent to use alone or mix with bait or lure.

Hog Ring Stake Connectors

Hog rings provide a fast and secure way to fasten trap chains to stakes, and 150 of them cost $2 at the local farm supply store. They are triangular and made from strong steel and copper. Use three at a time to be sure they hold.

Cattle Cubes for Cage Trapping Coon

When live-trapping raccoons, use cattle cubes or shell corn for bait. Raccoons relish both, but skunks, opossums, and other non-target varmints do not.

Recycle Post Hole Diggers into Trapline Shovels

When a post hole digger hinge wears out, unbolt the two halves, cut the handles down to about 30 inches and sharpen the blades with a file. Makes two great tools for digging big pocket sets and dirtholes; slices through small tree roots and pries out stones with ease.

Handy Trap & Trail Marking Clothespins

Instead of using surveyor's tape to mark trap sets and trails, spray paint clothespins fluorescent orange and you can just clip them onto brush or branches. After use, collect and use again.

WD-40 Makes Cage Traps Slick & Quick

When setting cage traps for small critters, first spray all joints and hinges with WD-40 to make them work slicker and quicker.

Pre-Cut Poplar Beaver Baits

Prepare spring beaver baits ahead of time by sawing poplar sticks into 15-inch lengths, with one end cut at a 45-degree angle to make it easier to push into the ground. Cut and partially peeled bait sticks may be bagged and frozen to stay fresh.

Blowtorch the Wax Off Trap Triggers

To allow trap triggers and dogs to engage properly after waxing, use a blowtorch to remove the wax at both contact points. One quick shot, and all is wax-free.

Rust-Free Snap Traps for Weasels

Snap-type rat traps work well for weasels, but they rust and leave marks on the fur. Wrap the striker bar with electrical tape, and it won't leave rust marks.

Cable Ties for Beaver Bait

When tying bait sticks to Conibears for under-ice trapping, instead of using wire, which is hard to get tight, use cable ties. Just pull tight with pliers and trim off the excess. Darken beforehand with a marker to make the tie less visible.

Lightweight Carry-In Trap Anchors

Put dry cement mix in empty gallon milk jugs and you can make drowning weights on site by simply adding water at the set and capping. For strength, make sure the handle fills with cement. If possible, get them out while scouting so the cement can dry ahead of time. You can easily carry a dozen or more with a rope looped through the handles.

Waxing Dirt for Trap Bedding

To make waxed dirt for bedding traps, set a sheet of black-painted plywood in the sun, spread a thin layer of dry sifted dirt (1/4- to 3/8-inch) on the board, and sprinkle flake wax onto the dirt. The black board absorbs and holds the sun's heat, causing the dirt to heat and the wax to melt; mix thoroughly until done.

Carve Your Own Fake Fox Droppings

A strategically placed fox dropping can enhance the effectiveness of a set. However, such droppings are not easy to come by, so carve decoy droppings from dry pine branches, about 3/8-inch thick and 1-1/2 inches long with both ends pointed. Dye in black Speed Dip for about 30 seconds, let dry, and use like the real thing. They work about as well and are easier to handle.

Q-Tip® Lure Dip Tip

Q-tips make great trapping lure holders. They can be dipped right in lure bottles with no mess or waste, cost little, are easy to carry in a shirt pocket or pouch, and really soak up the scent. Just stick a dipped Tip in the bank above a pocket set or slide set.

Place Bait Under the Cage Trap

Instead of putting bait inside a live trap where it may occasionally be taken without setting off the trap, scrape a shallow depression in the ground, put the bait in that, and then set the trap over top of it with the bait under the trap pan. This makes the animal reach down through the pan to get at the bait, which triggers the trap every time.

DIY Trapline Multi-Tool

For adjusting traps while out on the line, cut back the shank on a 3-inch file to 1/2-inch and ground it down to a flathead screwdriver tip. Not only do you have a file to clean unwanted wax and rust off trap dogs, but also a screwdriver. Drill a hole just behind the tip and attach a lanyard to keep it handy.

Lightweight Wire Spools

To make trapping wire easier to carry on the line, wrap just what you need on one of those lightweight plastic spools used for fishing line. Wrap the wire tightly around the middle, and it will not uncoil and tangle in your other gear.

Chop Tree Bark for a Quick Lure Holder

Before applying trapping or hunting scent to a tree, use a hatchet to make a chop up under the bark. Put the scent in this chop, and the bark cover will slow evaporation and also protect the scent from rain and snow.

Super Clean Trap Pack Baskets

To keep traps clean and scent free, make a pack basket out of a square plastic bucket with a snap-on lid. Cut a piece of 3/4-inch plywood for inside the bottom and attach straps with bolts and 1-inch washers. After drying, waxed traps go straight in the bucket, and the lid is then snapped on tight.

Duct Tape Claws to Prevent Pelt Damage

Before skinning a bobcat, lynx or fisher, wrap the feet with duct tape. Later, when you pull the feet through, the sharp claws will not damage the hide.

Oxygen Soap Takes Shine Off Snare Cable

The "oxygenated" powder soaps sold for laundry also do a great job preparing new galvanized snares to take on dye. I dyed mine with logwood crystals right after the cleaning, and even the locks and swivels, which were still bright metal, dyed just fine. Use a fragrance-free product.

Beaver Tail Makes a Handy Knife Strop

While skinning beavers, you may clean and strop your knife blade periodically on one of the leather-like tails.

Window Screen Rodent-Proofs Trap Bait

To prevent mice and shrews eating the bait at trap sets, wrap in metal window screen and wire it closed. The bait lasts longer, and you do not have to walk up to the set to check all of the time.

Magnetic Cage Trap Bait Holder

To secure bait to the metal pan of a cage trap, first set one of those flexible refrigerator advertisement magnets on the pan and then set a metal sardine can on top of the magnet to hold the bait.

Wax Traps in an Electric Cooking Pot

To dye and wax a few traps during the season, put them one at a time in an electric cooking pot (always available cheap at second-hand stores). Turn on high, and the wax melts quickly. When done, just unplug and put the lid back on the pot.

Hydrogen Peroxide Cleans Blood from Fur

To clean blood from fur, pour hydrogen peroxide directly on or dab it on with a rag and then wipe clean. Rinse thoroughly without delay as it may discolor the fur if left on too long.

Sticky Stuff Cage Trap Bait

Those sticky stump-licker deer attractors make great bait for cage-trapping raccoons. Toss some grass in the back of the cage and pour it on. For eye appeal, add corn. Small critters can't steal all of this bait, and when they drag a little out, it works as a trailing scent.

Aluminum Foil Bling-Bling Raccoon Set
A simple set for raccoons can be made by simply wrapping a trap pan with aluminum foil and setting it in 2 or 3 inches of water alongside the bank of a creek or farm pond. Raccoons grab at the shiny foil, triggering the trap.

Gooey Good Raccoon Bait
For a gooey good raccoon bait, mix equal parts honey and blackstrap molasses with a small bottle of imitation anise then add shredded cotton balls. To apply at the set, just twirl a stick in the jar.

Surplus Canvas Sandbags for Freezing Pelts
Army surplus canvas sandbags make excellent freezer bags for pelts. They last forever and only cost about $2.

Carpet Cleaner Takes the Funk Out of Fur
To get the funky smell out of a dried pelt that you would like to hang on a wall, sprinkle carpet cleaner on the leather and fur, let it sit for a week, then shake out and brush clean.

Dropper Bottles Handy for Scents
Use medicine dropper bottles to store, carry and dispense strong trapping, hunting, and fishing scents. Inexpensive at most pharmacies. Reduces mess and waste.

Clean Dirty Traps at the Car Wash
Take your dirty traps to the car wash. The high-pressure hot spray blasts away dirt, blood and mud.

Nut on Top Makes it Easier to Free Rerod Stakes
Instead of welding a washer near the top of a 1/2-inch rebar stake, drive the stake about 3/4-inch through a 5/8-inch nut and then weld that in place. When you need to pull the stake, put a wrench on the nut and give the stake a couple of turns to break

it loose. A bigger washer can be slipped onto the stake below the nut, if needed for a particular application.

Surplus Wool Liners for Warmer Gauntlets
Wear Army surplus wool liners inside gauntlets to keep hands warmer when trapping in cold water. They cost about $2 a pair.

Pin Fish Skin on Trap Pan for Attractor
When filleting fish, cut the skin into pieces a little larger than a trap pan and freeze. When making a water set for coon or mink, pin a piece of the skin right on the trap pan.

Pipe Cleaner Reusable Set Markers
Instead of using flagging to mark trap locations, use fluorescent-colored pipe cleaners. They are easy to see and easy to twist around a thin branch. Costs about the same as commercial flagging (when cut in thirds) but are much easier to reuse.

Use Super-Stout Wood Surveyor Stakes
For trapping stakes, ask a surveyor to order you some of the same stakes he uses. These are usually oak, ash or hickory, very stout, and only cost 30 to 40 cents each.

Salt Fish for Better Trapping Bait
Instead of freezing fish for trapping bait, salt them. Less messy, and after 3 years they still have a great fish smell. Just put a layer of salt in a 5-gallon plastic bucket, then a layer of fish (no need to gut them), a layer of salt, a layer of fish, a layer of salt, etc.

Garbage Bag Contains Cage-Trapped Skunk Funk
When setting a cage trap for skunks, slide a large black garbage bag over three-quarters of the back of the trap. This creates an inviting place for a skunk to investigate, keeps the bait dry should it rain, and also keeps the skunk calm as you walk up to the trap from the backside. If the little stinker does spray, pull the bag over the rest of the cage to keep the smell contained.

Make a Fake Attractor Egg from a Golf Ball

Where trapping regulations prohibit exposed baits, drill a hole in an old golf ball, fill the hole with lure, and you have a fake egg that isn't an egg but still a visual attractor. (Check first to make sure this is not illegal, too.)

Grocery Tote Serves as Trapline Dirt Bag

I carry dry dirt on the trapline in one of those canvas tote bags grocery stores now sell for a dollar or so. They can be used for traps and other supplies, too. When not in use, they fold up to fit in a pocket and can be cleaned by simply tossing in the laundry.

Styrofoam Allows Fine-Tuning of Float Sets

Cut 3/4-inch Styrofoam in 1-by-8-inch strips and tack one strip on the bottom of each side of a muskrat float. To fine-tune the floating depth, simply break off small pieces until the trap sits level, about an inch underwater.

Use Bread Bag Ties to Support Snares

Plastic-coated wire read bag ties make great snare supports: lightweight, strong and compact.

Kool-Aid Raccoon Trapping Scent

Berry or cherry Kool-Aid makes an economical raccoon trapping food scent lure. Spread on the ground at the set. Gives off a pungent, sweet odor, especially on misty nights when damp air wets the granules, releasing more scent. Must be replenished after a rain, but it's cheap and really works.

Add Plywood Skunk Guard to Cage Trap

Wire 1/4-inch plywood sheets to the top and sides of a cage trap and you can pick it up with a trapped skunk inside and not get sprayed. Very helpful for removing an animal from catch site.

Bulb Planter Speeds Dirthole Making

A bulb planter speeds up dirthole set making. Just push it in the ground at the desired angle, pull it out, and it punches a narrow, deep hole while also taking out the dirt.

Cedar Block Lets Muskrats Get Deep and Drown
Instead of trying to stake a muskrat trap out in deep water, attach a 6-inch block of 4-by-4 cedar post to the trap ring. Set the trap as usual and then drop the float at the edge in the water. Float and drowned rat are usually found in the nearest deep water.

Hang Bait in the Bucket
Before using a bucket to make a cubby set, drill a hole in the side of the bucket 6 inches up from the bottom. When making the set, tie the bait up with string and run the other end of the string through this hole, from the inside out. Position the bucket so the hole is on top, pull the string through until

Hang the bait in the top of a bucket cubby and it is more visible and harder to pilfer.

the bait dangles down about 2 inches, and then tie a small stick to the string on the outside of the bucket to keep it in position. The bait is more visible, and harder for rodents to pilfer.

Trap Setter Doubles as Tail Stripper
Pliers-type bodygrip trap setters may do double duty as tail strippers, especially when skinning out in the field.

Update Trap Tags with Mailing Label & Tape
Rather than throw away trap tags after a move, update with your new mailing address label and a wrap of clear packing tape.

Recycle CDs into Visual Attractors at Cat Sets
Old CDs make great visual attractors at bobcat sets. Glue two together, reflective sides out, and drill a hole to hang on a fine wire or fishing line. Include a fishing swivel, and it should spin in the lightest breeze.

Suet Sack Holds Cage Trap Bait

Wire a bird feeder suet sack in the back of a cage trap to hold the bait. When a critter can't reach in and steal the bait, it will likely enter the trap and then step on the trigger pan while trying to work the bait sack free.

Stake Down Cage Traps

When setting a cage trap, especially one with rings that slide down to lock the door shut, drive a long stake into the ground beside the trap leaving a foot sticking up above ground. Now wire the cage trap fast to the stake to prevent it tipping and the door possibly releasing.

Bed Traps Solidly on Aluminum Gutter Spikes

Lightweight aluminum gutter spikes are ideal for stabilizing traps in their beds. The spikes can be driven into 'most any surface vertically or horizontally, they don't rust and carry easily in an old videotape case.

Cut Back Hoe for the Trapline

To turn an old garden hoe into a great trapline tool, cut off the handle at a more compact carry length, run a grinder over the metal to knock off the rust and sharpen the blade. If the handle is rough, sand it smooth or wrap with tape. The hoe head is made for working dirt, and the end of the handle will quickly ream out a dirthole in loose soil or a pocket set in a muddy bank.

Engrave ID Numbers on Traps

In addition to always adding the required trap tag, engrave the last four digits of your social security number directly on the bottom of traps. Should you later catch somebody with the traps, you can positively identify them as your stolen property.

BBQ Tongs Ideal for Baiting Cage Traps

A pair of the long tongs made for grilling over a hot barbecue works great for placing bait in the back of a cage trap.

Spray Away Snarled Fur

To remove the snarly tangles in furs, apply children's hair detangling spray (found with the shampoo at the store). The tangles comb right out. Works great for dogs, too.

Sandbags Ideal for Drowning Sets

The sturdy sandbags made for flood control make ideal anchors for drowning sets. Just fill on site with rocks, sand or dirt.

110 Bodygrip Holds Pelts on Fleshing Beam

Wrap the jaws of a 110 bodygrip with black electrical tape and it makes a great clamp for holding open-skinned pelts on the fleshing beam. Just lay the pelt over the fleshing beam same as always and clamp the 110 jaws over the nose.

Bucket Handle Great for Cage Traps, Too

The sturdy wire handle from an old 5-gallon bucket works great on a cage trap, too. The hooks in the ends make it easy to attach to or remove from a cage. When you have a caged coon to move, hook the handle in the back of the cage, place your other gloved hand by the door, and it can be carried safely and securely.

Eggshells Add Instant Eye Appeal

Don't throw away eggshells; save them for the trapline. They offer great visual attraction for 'most any furbearer, and the cup shape makes a natural holder for fish oil or scent lure. (First check regulations regarding exposed bait where you trap.)

Brick Hammer a Great Trapline Tool

A brick hammer makes a great trapline tool, compact to pack in a basket yet stout enough for tough chores. Sharpen the blade side of the head to cut trap beds in sod, etc. Use the hammer side to drive stakes, and when pulling stakes, slide the blade side under the washer at the top of the stake and use it like a pry bar.

Horse Blanket Pins Handy for Pelts, Too

After skinning, put a blanket pin through the lower lip and up through the nose of a furbearer to help keep the pelt from sliding on the fleshing beam and also later on the stretcher. Also provides a handy way to hang a stretched pelt while it dries. A blanket pin is like a big safety pin, used for pinning horse blankets. They are inexpensive at tack shops.

Saving Cents on Trapping Scents

Pure almond extract makes a great muskrat lure. Sold at the grocery for less than trapping lure, effective, and easy to carry in the small glass bottle. Leftover bacon grease also makes a great scent lure. I carry that in a frosting jar.

Feed Bag Trapline Kneeling Cloth

Nylon feed bags make great scent-free kneeling cloths for making dirt sets. Lightweight, folds small, and any extra dirt can be carried away in the bag.

Cold Raccoon Pelts Easier to Flesh

When the outside temperature is below freezing, hang freshly skinned coon pelts outdoors until they just about freeze. They will flesh much cleaner without the dripping grease.

Hitch Pin Tail Stripper

A 3-1/2-inch hitch pin makes a good tailbone stripper for squirrel, mink, raccoon, fox and even coyote.

Carry Snares Tangle-Free in a Coffee Can

To prevent snares tangling, store and carry in 2-pound plastic coffee containers. Each one holds about 20 coiled snares; they stack and store neatly. Just be sure to thoroughly clean each container before use, to avoid scent contamination of the snares.

Toilet Plunger & Bucket Pelt Washer

To clean and degrease skinned pelts, fill a 5-gallon bucket halfway with warm water and laundry detergent, drop in the pelt, and then use a toilet bowl plunger like the agitator in a washing machine to work the pelts in the water. Much faster and easier than doing it all by hand.

Oxygenation Boosts Pelts, Too
Oxygenated laundry soap boosters clean hides better than plain detergent and leave the fur soft and shiny.

Color-Code Lure Bottles
Wrap color tape around bottles of trapping lure. Use a different color for each furbearer, and rather than putting on glasses to try to read a smeared label, the color will quickly tell which lure is which: red for fox, yellow for raccoon, etc.

.22 Short a Better Dispatch Round
A .22 Short point-blank to the head will dispatch a trapped animal as well as a .22 LR, but with less noise and also less bleeding because the slower bullet rarely passes through.

Cement Mixer Tumbles Old Dip, Rust from Traps
Remove rust and old trap dip by tumbling traps in a cement mixer. First remove the chains and tighten the pan screws. Then tumble with three-quarter minus gravel, either wet or dry.

Bar Clamp Trap Setter
A 21-inch bar clamp works well for setting 330 bodygrips or big longsprings, really any trap with a safety catch. Bar clamps are sold at hardware stores everywhere.

Cut Quick Trap Tags from Pop Cans
When you run out of trap tags, you can make some by cutting strips from an aluminum pop can. Lay the strip on rubber and then engrave/write on it with a ballpoint pen. Punch a hole to wire it to the trap chain and then roll it up.

Firewood Carrier Good for Lugging Furbearers, Too
A lightweight canvas firewood log carrier is ideal for one-hand carry of animals on the trapline. Nicely balances a 5-gallon bucket in the other hand.

Marshmallow Fluff a Raccoon-Only Bait

Marshmallow Fluff makes an effective raccoon-specific bait. Skunks, possums and pet cats are not at all attracted to it. Just dip a stick in the jar, and the sticky stuff won't come off. Stays in the pipe at PVC sets, too, giving raccoons a reason to work.

Shampoo Furbearers Clean

Pack a bottle of biodegradable shampoo when trapping near water. If a catch is muddy or bloody, dunk it in the water, shampoo, and rinse. Much less mess than hauling dirty critters back to the fur shed and then cleaning them there.

Shower Curtain Rings Make Great Bait Holders

Metal shower curtain rings are ideal for fastening chicken necks inside crab baskets (or cage traps). The wire punches through and holds the bait right where you want it. Easy to open and close; plated to last for years.

Zip Tie Hinges for Colony Traps

Small zip ties make excellent hinges for the doors on colony traps. They never hang up, open and close like greased lightning. Be sure to clip off tag ends. May also be used to quickly repair landing nets, seines, etc. Just thread the tie through the opposite corners of the damaged area and cinch tight.

Recycle Fan Blades into Stretcher Boards

Old ceiling fan blades are made of light wood and already close in shape to a fur stretcher board. A little trimming and sanding of the soft, lightweight wood may be all it takes to repurpose them for the fur shed.

Freeze Glands Before Lure Making

Deep-freeze glands and other animal parts for 30 days before using them to make lure. It helps kill the bacteria and germs.

Orange Duct Tape Trap & Trail Marker

Wrap orange duct tape around branches to mark trails and trap locations. It's faster and easier than tying surveyor ribbon, and just as easy to see later.

Color-Code Slider Cables
When making trapline drowner/slider cables in different lengths, use spray paint to color code the ends so you can tell length at a glance: 5-7 feet yellow; 8-10 feet white; 11-15 feet green, etc.

Fence Pliers the Original Trapline Multi-Tool
Fence pliers fill so many trapline needs perfectly. They quickly cut wire, crimp, pull staples; can even be used to pound a stake in the ground.

For Less Mess, Bait DP Coon Traps with Dry Cat Food
Bait dog-proof traps with inexpensive dry cat food. It comes in small pellets, is not messy but very effective.

Tough, Affordable Kneepads
The tough kneepads made for roofers and carpet installers are great for kneeling on the ground to make trap sets. The ones with hard-plastic kneecaps work best. They aren't expensive, and most hardware stores carry them.

Recycle Lunch Box as Bait & Lure Carrier
An old soft-sided lunch box is ideal for carrying bait and lure on the trapline. Most are lightweight, have an over-shoulder strap and zipper closure. Contains the smells and spills, and can be scrubbed clean.

Cement Reinforcing Mat a Multi-Use Fur Hanger
Rather than install dozens of ceiling hooks for hanging fur, put up one of the heavy wire reinforcing mats used in concrete work. More versatile, and it won't bend under a load.

Recycle Arrow Shafts as Belly Wedges
Bent aluminum arrow shafts make great belly wedges for small pelts like mink. Insert between pelt and wooden stretcher all of

the way to the lip. The fletching gives you something to pull. Cut to length, and sand any sharp edges.

VapoRub® Overpowers Fur Shed Odors

If the smells in your fur shed bother you, dab a little Vick's VapoRub under your nose to mask the odors.

Beaver Stick Scent Posts

The peeled sticks from beaver dams make great scent posts for trap sets. They come in all sizes, naturally aged and lightly beaver scented.

PVC Pipe Belly Wedges

Instead of cutting wood belly boards for my fur stretchers, I bought an 8-foot length of 1/2-inch gray PVC electrical conduit for $1.37 and cut that into 32-inch pieces. It won't break, splinter, mold or rot, costs half as much as hardwood, and can be wiped clean between uses.

Flea-Free Critter Cooler

Large but otherwise "retired" coolers are ideal for bringing home furbearers without the fleas or the mess in your vehicle. Line the bottom with newspaper. After dropping in a carcass, apply flea-spray and close the lid. When you get home, remove critters, newspaper, and then clean out the cooler with hot, soapy water.

Jerky Gun Great for Paste Meat Baits

A jerky gun makes a quick, clean and easy way to carry and use paste or ground-meat trapping baits. Ideal for getting the bait below the trigger of a dog-proof raccoon trap. Saves on waste.

Recycle Laptop Carry Case as Trapping Bag

Used laptop carry cases cost almost nothing at second-hand stores and work great as trapping bags. Most easily hold a dozen traps, pliers, lure, gloves, etc., in multiple compartments with heavy-duty zipper closure. A padded shoulder strap provides for hands-free carry.

Color-Code Snare Bundles
Twist ties work well for keeping snares tied up in neat bundles, and you can color-code the different sizes and lengths of cable by simply using different color twist ties.

Dry Seed Pod Lure Holders
Dry seed pods from sweet gum trees make great natural lure holders at trap sets. Hold the ball by the stem and dip it as deep as you like to apply the right amount of scent, which then pools inside the little openings to stay somewhat weatherproof.

Old Clothes Dryer Handy in the Fur Shed
An old clothes dryer comes in handy for drying wet hides. Most will dry 20 coon hides in about 20 minutes. Scrape the hides while they are still warm, and the fat glides right off.

Hemostats Also Handy in the Fur Shed
The locking hemostats commonly used to remove hooks from fish also may be used to hold the sides together when sewing up holes in furbearer pelts.

Fill Plastic Milk Jug with Sand for Small Fur Beam
Fill a gallon plastic milk jug with sand to make a handy fleshing beam for small furbearers.

Use Fishing Tube Lures in DP Raccoon Traps
The soft-plastic tube lures made for jig fishing can be slid over the triggers of dog-proof traps for a "feel" that raccoons cannot resist. Experiment with various colors and scents.

Powdered Gravy Mix at Raccoon Sets
For a good trail scent at coon sets, try inexpensive powdered gravy mix. Sprinkle in front of the set and behind then bait as usual with a favorite food lure.

Use Quick Link to Loop Trap Cable Around Tree
When using a cable extension to secure a trap to a tree, don't just

wrap the cable around the trunk and pass one looped end back through the other. Instead, wrap the cable around and use a quick link to hold the two looped ends together. Rigged this way, the cable won't cinch down but rather rotates freely around the tree, which could prevent an animal powering out of the trap.

Put Cage Bait in a Jar to Stop Pilfering

To stop rodents pilfering bait from a cage trap, place the bait in a clear plastic jar, add a shot of lure or fish oil, screw on the lid, and punch a few holes in the plastic to allow scent to escape. Makes the bait rodent- and weather-proof, and raccoons really go for something they can see and smell.

Wrap Tool Handles with Orange Tape

Wrap fluorescent orange tape (available at bicycle shops) around the handle of a trowel, hammer, and other tools used on the trapline. Saves tools from being left behind on the ground, and the tape may be removed at the end of the season.

Bucket Best for Shouldering the Load

For trapping in shallow water, make a shoulder bucket by removing the handle from a 5-gallon plastic bucket, melting two holes near the top of the bucket across from each other, and then attaching a shoulder strap. Duct tape a towel around the strap for padding. It's handier than a pack on your back and even floats in thigh-deep water to help carry some of the weight. While making a set, just stab a wading staff in the bank and hang the bucket on that.

Fly-Proof Aging for Trapping Scents

For a container to "age" trapping lure, fish oil, etc., punch or drill a hole through the screw cap of a large jar, sized so a 1/4-inch plastic hose connector (45 cents at the hardware store) can be screwed in. Then attach a length of the plastic hose (also at the hardware store) to this fitting. Put the other end of the hose at the bottom of a 1/2-gallon milk jug filled with water. As the bait "cooks," pressure vents through the hose, and the water in the second jug excludes flies or anything else from getting in.

Letter Opener Tail Splitter
Split tails easily with one of those square letter openers. The long stem leads the razor right down the tailbone. Companies often give them away as a promotional item.

Wrap Rope Around Springs to Set a Big Bodygrip
The springs on a large bodygrip trap may be set easily using 3 feet of 1/4-inch nylon rope. Tie a loop in one end to slip over the toe of your boot. Thread the other end of the rope up through the eyes of the spring. Go around the outside and thread up through the eyes a second time. Wrap around your hand and pull. This creates a mechanical advantage that easily compresses the powerful spring.

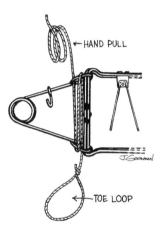

HAND PULL

TOE LOOP

Channel Lock Tail Stripper
A pair of channel lock pliers, fully opened so the handles come together, works great as a tail stripper.

Split Shot Keeps Cage Trap Doors Centered
To keep cage trap doors centered, crimp large split shot fishing weights tightly onto the wire as close to the hinge as possible, thus preventing the door sliding around.

Keep Trap Wire Tangle-Free in Trapping Bucket
Drill a 1/4-inch hole in the side near the bottom of a plastic packbasket or 5-gallon bucket. Lay a spool of trapping wire on its side by the hole, stick the end of the wire out through the hole, and bend down the end so it won't slide back inside. Keeps the wire handy and tangle-free.

Twist Pack Basket Straps for a Snug Fit

Twist the shoulder straps when putting them on a packbasket and they will better contour your chest and shoulders, since the twist forces them to the centerline. The twist also holds the straps open for easier in and out.

Trap Doubles as a Handy Stake Puller

To help pull a stubborn trap stake, use the trap. Close the jaws over the head of the stake and the welded-on washer won't let them slip off. Then the trap chain gives you something to hang onto while you pull.

Corncob Conibear Stabilizers

Old corncobs are ideal for stabilizing 110 Conibears on wooden lath stakes at muskrat sets. Slide the lath through the ring on the trap spring, and then wedge in a corncob.

Nursery Pot Makes a Great Conibear Cubby

Four-gallon landscaping nursery pots make great 220 Conibear cubbies. The groove around the top is just the right size to hold the corners of the trap jaw. Cut slits in the sides to hold the springs in place, angled down toward the ground for added stability. Drive a stake through the drain holes and into the ground to anchor the set.

Recycle Shower Curtain into Fur-Shed Apron

Make skinning aprons from old shower curtains by simply drawing a pattern and then cutting it out. Leave the grommets along the top to be used for a shoelace neck strap; punch a hole in each side of the apron for a waist tie.

Make a Stout Stake-Pulling Pole

Fourteen inches from the end of a 4-foot hardwood pole, install a heavy eyebolt to pry trap stakes loose. Place the near end of the pole on the ground, connect the trap chain to the eyebolt with an S-hook, and then lift the other end. I installed a screw hook in the other end so I could also use the same pole to pull trapped animals out of brush and traps out of muddy water.

Mailbox Mink Cubby
An old galvanized steel rural-delivery mailbox makes a great mink cubby. Remove the door (also cut off the back end if you prefer a tunnel) and cut slots for the trap springs.

Rebar Stake Fire Grate for Boiling Trap
To support a trap-boiling barrel over a fire, hammer eight or so rebar trap stakes straight into the ground in the right-size circular pattern and build the fire in the middle. The barrel sets on the stakes, and you can lower it by simply hammering the stakes deeper into the ground.

Vise Grips Good for Pulling Frozen Stakes
If a stake is frozen in the ground, clamp a pair of vice-grips on the stake nut and turn it while lifting and twisting. Any movement helps free the stake.

Veterinarian Needle Ideal for Sewing Pelts
The Loopuyt's needle veterinarians use to stitch up live animals also works great for stitching up a hole in a pelt. It is L-shape with a slight curve at the sharp end, making it easy to hold and push through hide. Ask your veterinarian where he gets his.

Railroad Plate Trap Drags
To make a raccoon-worthy water line trap drag from one of the flat steel plates used to connect railroad tracks, simply insert a pair of 4-inch-long 1/4-inch bolts through the holes at one end of the plate and secure with washers and nuts. The plate alone is heavy enough for mink, and the protruding bolts dig in to make it difficult for even the biggest raccoon to get far before hanging up in the brush.

Hollow Weeds Hide Bodygrip Trigger Wires
When setting bodygrips on land, cut hollow weeds with some branching and slide them over the trigger wires. Looks like all

of the other weeds, not a metal wire.

Pop Bottle Weasel Cubby
To make a lightweight cubby for weasel trapping, cut the bottom off of a 2-liter plastic soft drink bottle. To set the cubby, place a small piece of bait in the neck of the bottle and pull the chain of a No. 1 longspring (will fit in the bottle perfectly) through the bottle and out the threaded pour spout. After trap and bait are in the bottle, stabilize with rocks and place a couple of guide sticks out in front to direct a weasel in over the trap pan.

Recycle Garden Hose as a Skinning Knife Sheath
Skinning knives often do not come with sheaths because they are not intended for carry in the field. To protect the blade (and your fingers) cut discarded garden hose slightly longer than the blade and slide it on over the blade.

Coon Cage Trap Bait in a Can
When trapping raccoons with cage traps, place the bait in an old sardine can and wire it securely to the outside of the cage, near the top at the back with the opening accessible through the wires from the inside of the trap. Raccoons may reach over a pan trigger to steal bait placed at the bottom of a cage trap. But with the bait box secured at the top this way, they reach up and then step on the floor trigger.

Run New Traps Through the Dishwasher
To remove the factory grease from new traps, run them through a household dishwasher. Be sure the chains do not hang down to catch the rotating spray arm. The steel comes out grease-free and soon takes on a light coat of rust, ready for dye or dip. If you are worried about contamination in the dishwasher, run it again empty before using it for dishes.

Fishing & Boating

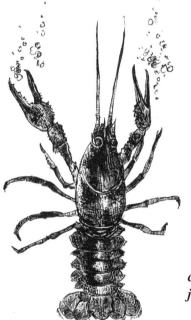

*"... when you see a
crawdad in shallow water,
just set the can over it and
it cannot scoot away."*

Coffee Can Crawdad Catcher

Crawdads make great fishing bait, but they can be
very difficult to catch by hand even in a small stream.
Cut the bottom out of a 3-pound metal coffee can, and
when you see a crawdad in shallow water, just set
the can over it and it cannot scoot away. Then you
may simply reach in and pick it up by hand.

Restore Metal Fishing Lures

To brighten tarnished fishing lures, wrap a cloth around the tip of a finger, dampen it, dip it in wood ash, and commence polishing. Wipe dry and admire.

Bag Minnows for Convenient Carry

A couple of dozen live minnows can be carried in a couple of cups of water in a gallon-size plastic bag. The bag will easily fit in a creel or even a large coat pocket, and the minnows will keep for hours. I'm not sure why this works so well, but it does.

Shop Vac Cricket Catcher

Crickets make great fishing bait but can be hard to catch. The next time you find them in your basement or outbuilding, put a clean bag in a shop vacuum and suck them right up. Remove the bag and drop the unharmed crickets into a cage, box, etc., by cutting a small hole in one corner of the bag. Repair the bag after each use by stapling the hole shut. Also helps to control insects in and around your home.

Flavor Ice-Fishing Baits

Add garlic powder to the little containers of maggots that are sold for ice-fishing bait. The garlic does not seem to hurt the maggots, but it does seem to make them more attractive to fish, especially crappies and trout.

Clip Hellgrammites to Reduce Snagging

Clip the back feet of hellgrammites so they cannot cling to the bottom or crawl as easily under rocks. Then run the hook up through the hellgrammite's collar. Or just cut off the head and collar, put the point of the hook in the tail, and turn the hellgrammite inside out over the hook for a grayish white glob that is often just what the fish want.

Spray Lead Sinker Molds with WD-40

Before use, lay a lead fishing sinker mold out open and spray with WD-40 to get rid of any unseen moisture. A little water in the mold can explode dangerously when the molten lead hits.

More than One Way to Skin a Cat(fish)
Pinch the barb closed on a large No. 4/0 stainless steel hook and attach 36 inches of heavy cord to hang catfish by the jaw for skinning. Tie to a rafter or loop around a tree limb. For safety, always take down and put away when finished.

Padded Car-Top Canoe Carry
To carry a canoe on top of your car, split the foam insulation made for hot water pipes and slip this onto the side rails. Simply cut out notches for any cross beams or oarlocks, and add a little bit of glue to hold it in place. It will not scratch the roof of the car, helps when portaging the canoe, and later, when you are fishing, it helps reduce the clunk of a paddle. I also find it serves as a handy holder for hanging fishing lures.

Ice Rod Does Double Duty on Backwoods Trout Ponds
To fish for trout in "back of beyond" Maine, I pack a 2-foot Zebco ice-fishing rod. Even in thick cover, it is easy to cast the 2-foot jigging rod. It came with a basic reel, was very affordable, and sturdy enough to stow behind the truck seat.

Dye Maggots for Eye-Catching Ice-Fishing Baits
Live maggots may be dyed to make more eye-catching ice-fishing bait by adding any food coloring you wish to a ball of hamburger and feeding it to them a day or two before the trip.

Bricks Make Good Ice-Fishing Foot Warmers
When ice-fishing, bring four bricks in the sled. Warm them on the stove in the fish house and then put two under your feet while you fish. As the two under your feet get cold, keep swapping them with warmer ones from the stove.

Catfish Love Frozen Liver-Pops
For a no-mess catfish bait, impale fresh chicken livers onto snelled 1/0 bait keeper hooks, place individual baits in the cups

of a small muffin tray, lay the snells over the sides, slide the tray into a plastic bag, and place in the freezer. To use, simply attach a snelled leader to your main line with a swivel snap. Baits stay frozen for hours in an ice cooler, and the frozen liver will stay on the hook and provide more than enough weight for casting.

Recover Snagged Lures with an Old Spark Plug
An old spark plug makes an effective retriever for snagged lures. Simply hook the spark end onto the line, hold the rod tip up and let it slide down to the snagged lure. If the initial bump doesn't knock the lure free, lift the rod tip up and down and the weight of the swinging spark plug may pull the snagged hooks free.

Recycle Arrow Shaft as a Fishhook Remover
Rather than discard a bent arrow, recycle it as a hook remover. Slice off the fletching and cut the shaft to a length of 6 to 8 inches, leaving the nock in place. To use, put the fishing line in the nock slot and slide the nock down the line to the curve of the imbedded hook. Push gently, and out comes the hook.

Free-Spooling with a Rubber Band
When tight-line fishing with slip sinkers, slip a rubber band around the handle of the fishing rod. After casting, reel in the slack and then pull a loop of line back and slip this under the rubber band. Open the bail of a spinning reel or push the release button on a bait-casting reel. When a fish takes the bait, the loop slips out from under the rubber band and the line pulls freely from the open spool. Increase the holding power in current by doubling up the rubber band.

Spill-Proof Pickup Truck Minnow Carrier
Place a car tire in the bed of your pickup truck and set a 5-gallon plastic bucket in the tire. Then, you can put a minnow bucket in the larger bucket and even on a rough road it won't tip, and any water or minnows that do slosh out will be contained in the 5-gallon bucket.

Pot Scrubber Doubles as a Fish Scaler

Use a metal dish-scrubbing pad to quickly and easily remove the small scales from trout and panfish. Hold the fish underwater and gently scrub each side. Then just rinse the pad.

Stock Up on Ice-Fishing Bait

During late summer, gather the abundant corn grubs and catalpa worms. Place in a large butter tub with a cup of corn meal and fill the rest of the container with damp sawdust. Kept in a refrigerator, the grubs and worms may live as long as six months. During ice season, when bait can be scarce, you'll be stocked.

Ketchup Cleanup for Fishy Hands

After cleaning fish, squirt ketchup on your hands, rub it in and then rinse in soapy water. Takes off the fish slime and eliminates some of the fishy odor the same way tomato juice helps get rid of skunk smell on a dog.

Diamond-Sharp Fishhooks

A fingernail file with industrial diamonds makes a great hook sharpener. File at a slight angle from the bend-over point, two times a side and once across the bottom. Inexpensive, and especially handy with small fly hooks.

Plump Up Night Crawlers

Put a dozen night crawlers in a 12-ounce cup. Dampen two paper towels and stuff them into the cup on top of the worms. Cover with a lid or aluminum foil and place in refrigerator a couple of days before going fishing. The worms will absorb the water from the towels, making them plumper and also more lively.

Corn Bait Holders

To prevent trout and other fish stealing corn bait, snip two pieces off of a yellow rubber grub body, each about the size of corn kernels, and thread one onto the hook over the eye. Now add a kernel of the real stuff and then impale the other rubber piece over the hook barb with the point just protruding through.

Canoe with Gear in 5-Gallon Buckets

When canoeing, stow sleeping bags and other gear in 5-gallon plastic buckets with closable lids. They keep gear dry and float should the canoe tip.

Dental Floss Box Pocket Tackle Tote

Dental floss boxes make excellent little carriers for fishing hooks, sinkers, swivels, etc., and the floss cutter built into the box does a fine job cutting light monofilament fishing line.

Pocket Ice Bait

After using up a stick of deodorant, clean the plastic tube and use it to carry maggots and wax worms when ice-fishing. Keep the tube in an inside pocket, and the bait will not freeze.

Fish Oil Makes a Good Catfish Sponge Bait

Sun-rendered fish oil and the finer stuff sold at trapper supply houses both work well as a catfish sponge bait and cost less than products sold to fishermen for the same purpose. You can render your own fish for free or buy the better oil in bulk from a trapping supply house.

Make an Ice-Fishing Live Well from a 55-Gallon Barrel

Drill many small holes in the lower half of a 55-gallon barrel, sink it in the ice of a lake, and it will keep shiners lively for the entire ice-fishing season. To keep it from falling through the ice, install four 10-inch carriage bolts 9 inches from the top. Secure with a nut and washer on both sides. When you need a minnow, lift the lid, break a hole in the thin ice that forms in the barrel and use a long-handled dip net. The minnows feed on food naturally in the lake water and stay acclimated. The best barrels for this are thick-walled plastic, curve in at both ends, and come with a snap-on lid.

Chalk It Up

Carpenter's chalk line (100-pound-test) is ideal for big pike through the ice. It won't cut on a sharp ice edge and doesn't cut into my hands as I fight a fish because it's about 1/8-inch thick.

Buckets Slow the Troll or Drift
To slow a boat to the desired trolling or drifting speed, tie a 5-gallon bucket to the outside corner of the transom and throw it overboard. Hang a second bucket off the other corner to slow it even more. When the buckets are not in use, they can be used to stow things.

Recycle Lunch Box into Worm Box
I bought a new lunch box for work and now use the old one for a worm bucket. It's lightweight, compact, and with a little bedding and a blue ice pack, it keeps night crawlers lively even on hot summer days. It's best to separate the worm bedding from the ice pack with a couple of layers of newspaper.

Insert Broom Handle in Boat Net
Put an old wooden broom handle into the hollow metal handle of a boat's fishing net. It will be stronger, and should it fall overboard, it will float.

Fillet Fork?
After using a fillet knife to cut the fillet from a fish, use a kitchen fork to pin the fillet to the table while removing the rib cage with the tip of the fillet knife. Leave the fillet on the table skin-side down, use the fork to pin down the tail, and you can easily "skin" the meat by sliding the fillet knife between the meat and skin.

Glue Foam Rubber Seat on Fishing Bucket
Glue a thick piece of foam rubber to the lid of a 5-gallon bucket to make a comfortable seat for fishing. The bucket itself can be used to carry minnows or left dry to carry in gear. After fishing, water can be added to carry the catch home. Keeps the fish alive and fresh for cleaning.

Recycle Car Floor Mats into Boat Mats
Take the floor mats from old junked cars and place them in the

bottom of your boat for a quieter, nonslip bottom.

Recycle Old Brake Rotors as Light Boat Anchors
Old auto brake rotors work well as light boat anchors, and most repair shops give them away. The best come from front-wheel-drive cars because they don't have a hub attached and you don't have to clean out any grease. Simply tie the anchor rope through one of the stud holes. The rotor lies flat on the bottom and "sets" with current or wind. They also work well as anchors for trotlines.

Pool Noodles Make Great Canoe Carry Pads
The "noodle" floating sticks kids use in swimming pools make great pads for carrying a canoe on a car top. Cut to size and split halfway through to slide over the gunnels. Cut shorter ones and use them to avoid sore shoulders when portaging. Scrap pieces can be tied to things that might sink if they fell overboard.

Cold & Lively Ice-Fishing Minnows
When setting up to ice-fish with minnows, put a little ice or snow in the bucket to acclimatize the minnows. They will not be as shocked when they hit the cold lake water and will be more lively on the hook.

Recycle Wrapping Paper Tubes as Fishing Rod Tubes
Save the tubes gift wrapping paper comes on and use them to store/carry two-piece fishing rods. You can leave the reel on, even leave hooks on the line without tangling.

Cedar Block Fishing Lure Hanger
Attach a small block of cedar to the side of your boat to hold lures while fishing. The lures are always at hand, and the soft wood doesn't dull the hooks.

Use Old Toothbrush & Paste to Clean Lures
An old toothbrush with a bit of toothpaste quickly cleans fishing lures without damaging the finish. The mild abrasive takes away

the grime but not the shine.

Bring Tackle to the Spearing House
When spearing pike in an ice shanty, bring a thread spool with enough fishing line wrapped around it to reach the shallow lake bottom. A light gold hook tied to the end and baited with whatever the fish like may get you a mess of panfish, and the activity may even attract a pike for the spear.

Walleye Cheek Meat a Treat
Slice out the cheek meat when you clean a mess of walleyes. Remove from skin, boil and serve with melted butter or a hot sauce dip. The cheek meat is delicious, way too tasty to be thrown away.

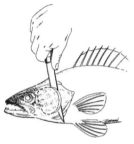

Use the Ice Chips for Sure Footing
To keep from sliding on slick ice while hand-augering a hole for ice-fishing or trapping, lift out the ice chips as they form and spread them on the ice underfoot.

Scale Fish Underwater for Less Mess
When using a scraper-type fish scaler, hold the fish by the head underwater in a 5-gallon bucket while you work; the scales seem to come off easier and don't fly everywhere. When done, pour the water on plants for free fertilizer.

Car Heater Takes Out Fly Leader Kinks
To work out the kinks in a tapered fly leader, set the car heater between medium and high, pull the leader straight and hold it about 1-1/2 inches away from the vent for 10 or 15 seconds. The leader should "relax" and be good as new after it cools.

Use Jumper Cables to Hold Boat
Split a set of old battery jumper cables in half lengthwise and you get two handy fishing boat or canoe holders, one for each

end. When you want to stay put and fish a hole, snap the gripper end to a root, limb or anything else that may be handy. No tying or untying needed.

Ice Cooler Keeps Minnows Lively

An ice cooler works great for keeping minnows lively on summer days, and you don't have to worry about the water freezing while ice-fishing. Also doubles as a fishing seat.

Nail Polish Brush Bottle Ideal for Fishing Scents

Clean empty fingernail polish bottles with solvent and then soapy water to make great holder/applicators for fish-attracting scents. The bottle fits easily in a pocket, and the brush on the cap works great as an applicator, applying scent to lures with little or no waste.

Put Small Hooks in Tic-Tac Box

Remove the top from an empty Tic-Tac box and fill with small fishhooks—a separate container for each size hook. Put the plastic top back on, put a piece of tape on the container and write the size of the hook. Same as the mints, hooks shake out of the flip-top lid one at a time.

Water Bottle Plumps Up Night Crawlers

Put night crawlers in an insulated water bottle without any dirt. Fill the jug with water and ice, and the crawlers will soak up the water until they are as plump and lively as they can get. As long as you keep ice in the water, they won't die even sitting in the sun on a 90-degree day.

Sand in Coffee Can Makes Leeches Easier to Handle

Before trying to put a leech on a hook, drop it in a coffee can of dry sand for 10 seconds. The stunned leech curls up and is easier to impale on a hook.

Insulated Water Jugs Keep Minnows Lively

One-gallon insulated water jugs are easy to pack, and with a little ice will keep dozens of minnows lively on the hottest day.

Align Minnow Traps with the Current

When setting a minnow trap, align it with the current so the minnows naturally enter while following the trail of bait upstream. When you have plenty of minnows and want no more, turn the trap crosswise to the current. The minnows will still face into the current, but now crosswise to the trap opening so none will accidentally back out.

Save the Anchor Rope

If you run the rope through the anchor and back to the boat, should the anchor become hopelessly stuck, you can at least untie and pull back the entire rope.

Milk Jug Bluegill Keeper

Cut a hole near the top of a gallon milk jug and fill it half full of water. As you catch bluegills, just drop them in the jug. They can't flop out, and it is much faster and easier than putting them in a basket or on a stringer. Simply dip the jug in the pond to refresh the water periodically.

Brick Dust Turns Night Crawlers Bright Red

For the brightest red night crawlers you've ever seen, pulverize red brick and put the dust in with them for a week or so. The color is proven to trigger bites.

PVC Cement Quick Fix for Inflatable Boat, Waders

For fast repair of inflatable boat leaks, pack a bottle of PVC cement (available at any hardware store for $2). Just clean the surface and apply directly to the material. Dries rock hard within 30 minutes. Also works well patching small holes in waders and repairing cracked bobbers.

Winter Worm Storage

In the fall before the ground freezes, dump your hoard of earthworms, including the dirt, in a pile on the ground; they will be back in the same place come spring.

Vacuum Pack Fish with a 5-Gallon Bucket
Fish fillets may be vacuum-packed in sealable plastic storage bags using nothing more than a 5-gallon bucket of water. Fill a bag with fillets and then slowly lower the bag into the water with the open end on top. Pressure from the outside water pushes the sides of the bag in and the air out the top. Then simply seal shut.

Use Power Drill to Strip Old Line Off a Reel
To make a tool for quickly stripping old line off of fishing reels, drill a hole in the bottom center of a metal coffee can, insert a bolt with washer from the inside, tighten down with a washer and nut on the outside, and then insert the end of the bolt into a power drill's chuck and tighten. After you power wind the old line onto the can, it can be slipped off and discarded properly.

A Stitch in Time Saves Minnow Net
Before using a new minnow net, stitch around the frame with fishing line. Holds the mesh to the frame before it unravels.

Newspaper Bag Keeps Reel Lightly Oiled and Clean
After cleaning and oiling a fishing reel, I put it back on the rod, slip a plastic newspaper bag over the rod handle and reel and secure with a wrap of tape. When opening day rolls around, the reel is still lightly oiled, dust and moisture free.

Styrofoam Tackle Box Insulation
To help prevent the summer sun melting plastic baits in your tackle box, glue a sheet of Styrofoam on the underside of the lid. Insulates and also doubles as a hook holder.

Golf Club Sleeves Also Good for Fishing Rods
The plastic tubes golfers put in their bags to separate clubs are also good for protecting fishing rods. If one is not long enough, simply duct tape two end to end. The tubes are tough enough to prevent even a klutz snapping off a rod tip or line guide.

Needle Nose Handles Open Jammed Jar Lids

The lids on old jars of pork trailers tend to stick over time because of the saltwater. But if you carry needle-nose pliers in your tackle box, you may turn them around and use the curved handles to grip the lid and open it more easily.

Lemon-Fresh Frozen Fish

Before storing fish in the freezer, place them in a container with water and add a little lemon juice to the mix. The frozen water seals the fish to prevent freezer burn, and the lemon juice adds a nice flavor.

Duck Decoys Double for Jug-Fishing

Floating duck decoys work great as jugs for turtling or catfishing. Just wrap the drop line around the decoy body and write your name and address on the bottom with a permanent marker. Wire a light stick to the neck for night fishing or paint old decoys fluorescent orange for easier viewing at night. Easy carry with the decoy bag.

Fingernail Polish Fishing Spoon Make-Over

Refurbish tarnished or just plain old fishing spoons with glitter fingernail polish. Once the polish dries, put the spoon on a flat pan in a preheated oven for about 20 minutes at 350 degrees. This bakes on the finish, though you still may want to stow the nail polish bottle in the tackle box for quick touch-ups.

Matchbook Spinner Holders

Matchbooks make good holders for small spinners tied with leaders. Keep a portion of the spinner blade exposed so you don't have to unwrap it to check the color.

Collect Crawlers Day and Night

To collect night crawlers during the day, dissolve a tablespoon of dry mustard in a pint of water. Find the mud cap top of a worm's hole, remove it, pour a little of the mustard water down the hole, and the worm will crawl out. Drop the night crawler in fresh water to rinse it off before putting it in the bait container. Wet the ground first, and you will need less mustard water.

Basketball Net a Slam Dunk Boat Anchor
A nylon basketball net makes a great anchor for a canoe or small boat. Carry the net with a rope in the boat. Before launching, pick up a heavy rock suitable for the conditions and put it in the net. At portages, simply drop the rock and replace it when you get back to water.

Egg Carton Keeps Small Reel Parts Organized
When taking apart a fishing reel (or other small but complicated item) use an egg carton to keep the parts organized. Number the egg-holder cups 1 through 12. Put the first piece in 1 then continue with 2, 3, 4, etc. When putting it back together, just reverse the order: 12, 11, 10, etc.

Wash "Fishy" Hands with Mouthwash
To eliminate "fishy" odors, wash your hands in mouthwash. It's a disinfectant, too, and generic off-brands are not expensive.

Keep Jumper Cables in Your Boat
Carry a set of jumper cables in your electric-start boat. If the battery goes dead, a fellow boater may give you a jump and get you back on your way. It is not easy to hand-crank a cold outboard. To prevent a dead battery in the first place, install a voltmeter, which typically sells for less than $20.

Keep Ice-Fishing Minnows in an Insulated Jug
When ice-fishing, keep the minnows in a wide-mouth insulated picnic jug. The wide mouth accommodates a net to remove the minnows, and the insulation prevents them freezing.

Make a Boat Net Float with Styrofoam Peanuts
Fill the hollow metal handle of a boat's fish landing net with peanut-shaped Styrofoam packers. It will float even if you drop it overboard.

Jar Lid Opener Also Straightens Leaders

Circular rubber jar lid openers work well for straightening fishing leaders. Simply fold a piece around the leader and pull along its length. The tension removes any line memory, and the leader is ready to fish. They come several to a pack for less than a dollar, and they can be cut to fit a leader case or vest pocket.

Wet Line Spools Easier

When putting fresh line on a fishing reel, place the plastic spool of line in water before you start reeling. The spool will spin freely in the water, and the line will come off tangle-free.

Paint Toughens Up Styrofoam Minnow Bucket

Apply outdoor paint on the bottom half of a Styrofoam minnow bucket to add toughness where most leaks occur.

Gut Fish to See What They've Been Eating

When you catch a fish you plan to keep, gut it immediately to check the contents in its stomach. Now you can pick lures or baits to match, and the gutted fish can go on ice.

Expanding Foam Easy Way to Add Flotation to Boat

To add flotation to the enclosed ends of a boat, drill two small holes into the hollow compartment—one at the top, one at the bottom—and fill with the spray expanding foam insulation sold at hardware stores. Just push the spray can tube in the bottom hole and spray until foam comes out the top hole. Dries in about 10 minutes and works great.

Winter Jug Fishing

We use old milk jugs to ice-fish for northern pike. Tie 20 feet of stout line to the handle. Set the bait to the depth you want and then walk away with the jug until the line is tight. When a pike takes the bait, the jug takes off toward the hole. Grab the line and set the hook. On windy days, just lay the jug downwind of the ice hole.

Spearhead Makes a Hard-Hitting Frog Gig

For a better frog gig, use a fish spearhead instead of a frog spear. Fish spears are bigger, more heavily built, and last about 10 times longer. For the pole, forget broom handles. They are heavy and slow the strike. Instead, use 6 feet of bamboo. The finished gig will be light as a feather yet hit like a tank.

Salt Those Salmon Eggs

Sprinkle a little table salt into a salmon egg container to toughen up the skin on the eggs; salt attracts fish, and the eggs will stay on the hook better.

Can't "Beat" This for Removing Old Fishing Line

Use an electric kitchen mixer to quickly remove old line from a fishing reel. Just insert one beater and tie the line to it. Start slowly and then speed up. Empties most reels in about a minute.

Instant Hand-Tied Fishing Fly

To make a quick wet fly, swab cement on the shaft of a fly hook of proper size, wrap with white pipe cleaner to the desired girth, and then paint on a black or brown head to mimic a grub.

Spread Sand on Ice for Better Traction

Bring a coffee can of sand when you go ice-fishing. Sprinkle some around the holes and on the paths in between to prevent slipping. The plastic snap lid prevents sand spilling in transit.

Waxed Ice Augers Work Best

Wax the bottom 6 inches of an ice-fishing auger blade to keep down the ice buildup and improve cutting performance.

Tip Ice Jigs with Just the Minnow's Head

When ice-fishing with a jigging rap, don't put a whole minnow on the bottom treble hook. Instead, pinch off just the head and put that on the front hook. Start the hook through the bottom of the head and push out the bony top.

Utility Knife Ideal for Cleaning Turtles
A utility knife (also known as a drywall knife) works great for cleaning snapping turtles. Put in a sharp new razor blade and it easily cuts the skin around the shell. Then use pliers to pull off the skin, and the meat will be very clean.

Kerosene Lantern Best for Collecting Night Crawlers
When a bright flashlight hits a night crawler, it may shoot back in its hole. But a kerosene lantern gives enough light without spooking the worms, and it also lights a bigger area.

Plastic Fork Helps Catch Night Crawlers
To pick up night crawlers, use a plastic fork with the tines sanded down to make them thin and somewhat pliable. Just slide the fork under the worm, put a finger on the worm to hold it on the fork, and lift. Works especially well on wet asphalt or concrete.

Catch the Nippers with a Hook in Worm's Tail
When fish are nipping at the tail of a rubber worm, slide as much of the worm as you can over the hook and up onto the line and then rehook the worm back near the tail. Works with live night crawlers, too.

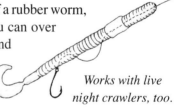

Works with live night crawlers, too.

Collect Cheek Meat with a Grapefruit Knife
A curved grapefruit knife is ideal for removing the delectable cheek meat from walleyes. Works for everything from perch to large pike. Just touch up the edge with a fine mill file.

Water-Filled Pans Catch Grasshoppers
To catch grasshoppers for fishing bait, simply place pans of water in the tall grass. But check often as birds soon get wise to the free lunch.

Lanyard Keeps Fishing Tools Handy
Fasten a pair of forceps (for hook removal) and nail clippers (for

cutting line) to a double duck-call lanyard and wear it around your neck while fishing. Your two most used tools will be handy all the time, and you can just loop the lanyard around your tackle box handle to store between trips.

Sandy Fingers Better for Catching Night Crawlers

When collecting night crawlers, bring a can of fine sand and every so often dip your fingers in the sand. With the extra traction, crawlers will be easier to pull out of their holes and you won't have to pinch so hard they break.

Liquid Truck Bed Liner Good for Boats, Too

The liquid liner sold for pickup truck beds may also be used to seal the rivets and small cracks in an aluminum johnboat. A can costs about $30 and seals two 12-foot boats. All you have to do is rough up the surface a little then brush it on. It's tough stuff that holds up well in all conditions.

Fill Push Pole with Expanding Foam

I filled a flat boat aluminum push pole with expanding spray foam insulation. Now it floats and is more rigid. To fill the pole, I used a plastic hose that fit on the spray can and was half as long as the pole. Worked it from the middle to the end then did it from the other end, too. When duck decoys get shot up, fill them with the foam and they will keep floating, too.

Keep Your Crawlers Cool

On hot days, keep night crawlers lively by putting a sealed plastic bag of ice in the bait container under the dirt. Keeps the dirt cool yet dry and the worms ready for action.

Rub Fishing Rod Ends on Your Nose

Before you put together a breakdown fishing pole, roll all of the "male" connector ends on the outside of your nose. The natural skin oil will lube them just enough that they won't stick later when you want to take the rod back apart.

Shaving Cream Cleans Fish Stink Off Hands
Keep a small travel-size can of scented shaving cream (menthol works best) in your tackle box and use it to clean the stink off of your hands.

One-Man Ice-Fishing Windbreak
The plastic sled you used to haul in your ice-fishing gear also works as a one-man windbreak. Stand it up and hold it in place with a bungee cord around your 5-gallon bucket seat.

Keychain Light Ideal for Tying Tackle at Night
When night fishing, tie a keychain light on a loop of string that will hang loosely around your neck. Best is the kind with a pressure switch for a quick check of line or hook and also an on-off switch for lengthier knot tying. My favorite has a red LED bulb that is plenty bright enough yet does not attract bugs.

Use Safety Pin to Open Split Rings
Open a split ring connector with a safety pin by pushing the point of the pin in between the first and second rings to pry them open. Now you can thread on the hook or lure.

Make a Fly Case from an Old Eyeglass Case
To make an excellent fly case, one designed and sized to fit nicely in a shirt pocket, simply glue a piece of sheep's skin into a clam-style eyeglasses case.

5-Gallon Bucket Canoe Ballast
When canoeing alone, bring a couple of empty 5-gallon jugs. Fill with water and place in the front of the canoe to provide stabilizing ballast. When done, empty back into the lake.

Net Shad at the Boat Ramp
If you want to net shad for bait, drive down a boat ramp on a calm night. Put your lights on dim, wait a few minutes, and let the light attract shad within easy range of a cast net.

Chicken Skin Fishing Bait

The tough skin from the lower part of a chicken leg can be cut into wax worm-sized pieces to make a great fishing bait. Fluttering on an ice fly, it works better than the real thing, and one tough piece may catch a dozen fish. Bluegills and crappies can't get it off of the hook like a wax worm. The more yellow in the skin, the better it seems to work.

Needle Threader Also Good for Threading Hooks

A needle threader from a sewing kit works just as well for threading fishing line through small hook eyes, and a pack of three costs about $1.

Speedy Way to Drain Water from a Johnboat

When a johnboat without a pump fills with rainwater, fire up the outboard and pull the rear drain plug while running across the lake at speed. As the water drains the boat nose lifts until the bottom is completely empty. Just don't forget to put the plug back before slowing down.

Collecting Grasshoppers at Night

Don't waste time chasing grasshoppers for fishing bait. Instead, wait until night and walk a field edge checking the brush with a flashlight. The docile grasshoppers will be as easy to gather as blackberries. To carry them without any escapes, use a 3-pound coffee can with a small flap cut in the plastic lid. Drop the hoppers in headfirst. When done collecting, duct tape closed.

Know the Line Weight

Stick a small adhesive label on a fishing reel (cheap at an office supply store) when you change the line. Write the brand, test weight, and date on the label. Helps to select the right line/rig for the type of fishing planned and also tells when the line is old and should be replaced.

Use Rubber Band for Split Shot Dropper Line

A piece of rubber band makes an ideal dropper for split shot.

Use a barrel swivel to connect the hook leader to the main line and tie the rubber dropper to the front loop of the swivel. If you snag, "pop" the line and the elastic helps jiggle the shot free. If it doesn't come loose, the rubber breaks saving the rest of the rig.

Deep Box Screens Out Weak Worms
Make a deep worm box, and after you stock it with night crawlers, wait several hours then pick the ones off the top for first use. The healthy ones will burrow deep. Using the weak ones first reduces the risk of rotting crawlers ruining the whole batch.

Fly-Line Dressed with Vinyl Protector Casts Farther
To cast farther, clean fly-line with soapy water, dry, and then apply auto vinyl protector—the kind used on a car's dashboard—with a damp rag. Also do the eyes on the rod.

Minnow Basket Leech Trap
To catch fishing bait, put liver or hamburger in the basket of a minnow bucket (the part with the small holes). Sink in a pond with leeches and leave overnight. Leeches squeeze through the holes to get at the meat but cannot get out quickly enough when you pick up the bucket in the morning.

Dip Flies in Seafood Broth
Next time you boil shrimp, lobsters or crabs, dip fishing flies and lures in the leftover broth. If you aren't a seafood chef, make them more enticing by dipping in cod liver oil, inexpensive at all pharmacies.

Surveyor Tape Makes a Boat Channel Safer
Where trees and brush wash into a lake, tie fluorescent surveyor tape to the bad ones. Then, when boating out after dark, shine a light to see and miss them with the boat.

Super Little Tackle Scissors
The small thread scissors sold at fabric stores are ideal for fly tying, cutting braided fishing line, and snipping to alter soft

plastic baits. Also good for skinning small game, so pack a pair with your hunting gear, too.

Make Your Own Scented Steelhead Lures

Heat 3.75 ounces of petroleum jelly until liquid, pour in 1 ounce pure anise oil, and stir well. While mix is still liquid, drop in tiny yellow and orange sponges. Pull them out, and after the jelly hardens the scent will be locked in. The scented, colored sponges also make dynamite attractors at muskrat sets.

Aerate Minnow Bucket with Inner Tube

For driving long distances, make a portable aerated minnow tank with a truck tire inner tube, 4 feet of rubber hose (sized to fit snugly over the inner tube valve stem), a hose clamp, and a 5-gallon bucket. Slightly overfill the inner tube and then slide it over the bucket. Now, use a valve stem remover to open the valve just a little, push the hose over the valve stem, clamp it on, and drop the other end of the hose into the bucket. Provides hours of silent aeration, with no batteries. Can also use your vehicle's spare tire but remember to bring an air pump to top off the spare after you arrive.

Dough Better than Bread for Baiting Minnow Trap

Use raw bread dough instead of baked bread to bait a minnow trap. Baked bread falls apart and floats out of the trap; dough stays put as it dissolves, and the minnows go inside to get it.

Knot Stops Split Shot Slipping Down the Line

To prevent split shot slipping down the line to the hook, tie a simple square knot at the desired distance above the hook and it will stop the shot sliding.

Erasing Bad Line Memories

Fishing leader stored on a spool can develop memory curl. You can remove this with a 1/8-inch groove cut across a rubber pencil eraser. Place the leader in the groove, pinch the eraser together, and pull the leader through.

Shine Lures with a Pencil Eraser

Keep a rubber pencil eraser in your tackle box to remove surface grime and tarnish from metal spinner blades and spoons. Does a good job without scratching the finish.

Mirror Makes Trailer Hook-Up Easy

Mount a mirror on the front of your boat trailer, tilted so you can look in the mirror when seated in your tow vehicle and see the trailer hitch. It will make it much easier to back into the right hook-up position.

Coat Dough Balls with Corn Meal for Less Mess

Form dough fishing bait into bait-sized balls, roll the balls in corn meal, and keep the coated balls in a wide-mouth jar with a lid. They will stay fresh and be less messy to use.

Two-Lidded Can Best for Easy Worm Retrieval

Make the ultimate worm can out of two coffee cans with snap-on plastic lids. Cut the bottom out of one, take the plastic lid off the other and put it on the bottom of the one you just cut. Fill with dirt and worms. When you want a worm, turn the can over, take off whichever lid is on top, and the worms will be on top, too.

Waste Not, Want Not Fishing Line

Spinning reels often hold more line than you really need, and if you do go deep into the spool, you lose casting distance. So, before loading the reel, wrap layers of thick tape around the spool to decrease the line capacity. When you do change line, there will be less waste.

Use Scented Foam Rubber for Minnow Trap Bait

When trapping minnows, don't use food bait because the minnows will overeat and then make waste in the storage tank, which is unhealthy for them. (A red ring around a minnow's eyes indicates this.) Instead, soak 1-inch cubes of foam rubber in fish or chicken broth. The scent lures minnows into the trap but leaves their stomachs empty.

Tarnished Brass Best for Spooky Trout

Trout may be spooked by a too-flashy spinner blade. So, bury a couple in the dirt until the brass tarnishes and use those for the "spooky" rainbows.

Rubber-Coat Trailer Hook Eyes for Easy Rigging

To be able to quickly add trailer hooks to lures, dip the eyes of the trailer hooks in a flexible adhesive (the kind used to patch waders). When the coating dries, you can push the hook eye on over the barb of another hook and it will not shake off.

Get a Gator Grip when Filleting Fish

Clip a jumper cable alligator clip to the mouth of a slippery panfish before filleting. It really helps to have something that isn't slippery to hold onto.

Bleed Out Big Fish for Better Taste

To greatly improve the flavor of large fish, cut the tail while the fish is alive and let the fish bleed out. To get rid of the fishy smell on your hands, wash with milk.

Empty Water Bottle Keeps Boat Bag Afloat

Leave an empty plastic water bottle in your canoe or kayak kit bag. If you turn over, the bag will not sink.

Clean Panfish on a Clipboard

A plastic clipboard with a stout clamp works perfect as a fillet board for panfish. The clamp holds the fish, and the plastic board cleans easily with just soapy water. Store it in the same plastic bucket where you put the fish you catch.

Pop-Up Blind Also Good for Ice-Fishing

After deer season, my pop-up hunting blind does double duty as a portable ice-fishing shanty. It is the right size for sitting and fishing, doesn't have a floor so I can just peg it to the ice over an ice hole, and the shooting port lets me look out to check other tip-ups.

Carry Crickets in a Cheese Shaker

Carry live cricket baits or mealworms in an old Parmesan cheese canister. Poke a few small holes in the side for air then place tape over the shaker holes leaving only one open for shaking out crickets/worms. When you need one, just turn the top to open this one hole and shake it out. Add a piece of parachute cord as a carry strap; reinforce with duct tape, and it may last more than one season.

Shotshell Oarlock Tightener

To tighten a loose oarlock on a rowboat, cut the brass end off an empty shotshell and then cut a slit lengthwise in the plastic hull, leaving 1/2-inch uncut. Curl the cut end, insert this into the lock, and gently tap it down. Now slide in the oarlock pin. No more squeaking, and the oar stays put in the oarlock.

Hot Idea for Hooking Plastics

To prevent soft plastic worms and other lures sliding down the hook and balling up after a cast or strike, heat the hook with a butane lighter. First, hook the lure but do not push it up the shaft of the hook. Now heat the shaft of the hook for a few seconds and then immediately push the lure up the hot shaft and into place against the hook eye. The plastic melts, causing it to grip.

Hook Big Baitfish Headfirst

Always hook a big baitfish in the top of the head, because predatory game fish take them headfirst.

Blood Bait Chum for the Turtle Trotline

Next time you set a turtle trotline, bring a container of the blood bait sold for catching catfish. Roll it into marble-sized balls and disperse it around the baited hooks. Draws in turtles like a charm.

Add a Bobber so Dropped Jaw Spreaders Won't Sink
Jaw spreaders are great for removing lures from toothy pike, but they sink if dropped overboard (which happens). To avoid this, attach a big bobber to the spreaders with a piece of cord.

Stain Cork Rod Handles Dark to Hide the Dirt
Before using a new cork handle fishing rod, stain the cork dark oak or pine and it will never show dirt. If it's a two-piece rod, wrap a rubber band on the handle right below the reel. When you disassemble the rod, put the tip of the top section through the large guide on the butt section of the rod and then slide the rubber band over the other end. Leave the rubber band on the rod seat and it will always be handy.

Tilex® Great for Cleaning Boat Hulls
To keep a boat clean and also help control the spread of unwanted invasive species, spray the hull with Tilex every time you take it out of the water. It gets into the tight places and leaves the hull shiny clean without scrubbing.

Kayak Paddle for the Canoe
To paddle a canoe continuously instead of with only half of each stroke, use a double-bladed kayak paddle.

Two-Liter Minnow Trap
A two-liter plastic pop bottle can be made into a small minnow trap by simply cutting off the top end, turning it around and sticking it back in the bottle to make a funnel-like opening. Add bait and place where minnows school.

Fillet Fish on the Paddle
When on a backcountry canoe trip, fillet the catch right on the canoe paddle.

Solar Lawn Lights Good for Night Fishing
The solar-charged lights that people stick in their lawns also work great for night fishing — and you never need to buy batteries.

Use Pipe Cleaner to Feed Baitcaster Line

Trying to feed monofilament line through the level-wind guide on a bait-casting reel and then around the spool to be tied on can be difficult, but a pipe cleaner makes it much easier. Just wrap the line around one end of the pipe cleaner, fold it over, and then use that to thread the line through and around.

Pay Less for Cricket Baits at a Pet Store

If you need fishing bait in a pinch, try a pet store that sells reptiles. They usually sell live crickets for about a dollar a dozen.

Tip Jigs with Tongues

If you run out of minnows, cut out the tongues of the crappies you already have on ice (the area beneath the gills forward to the back of the lower lip). Tip a jig with a tongue, work it slowly, and it "swims" like a live minnow.

Duct Tape Trout Net on a Longer Handle

Lash a small trout landing net to the end of an old broomstick with duct tape to make a longer-handled net for the deep pools. Also doubles as a sturdy wading staff.

Heat Hooks to Make Them Easier to Pull Free

Take the temper out of thin wire crappie hooks by heating them with a lighter. Crappies won't straighten out the weakened hooks, but when one snags a log, it can be straightened out by simply pulling on the line. Bend the hook back the way it was and keep on fishing without changing any tackle.

Put Refrigerator Magnets in Tackle Box Trays

Cut thin refrigerator magnets to fit and glue them in the trays of a tackle box. The magnets hold small hooks and other steel tackle so they don't spill out.

Use Clothesline to Show How to Tie Fishing Knots

Use cotton clothesline when showing someone how to tie a fishing knot. Much easier to see than thin monofilament fishing line, and also easier to tie.

Let the Drive Home Wash Out the Live Well
After putting the fish on ice in a cooler for the ride home, fill the boat live well half full of clean water and squirt in a little dishwashing detergent. The drive sloshes the water around and really cleans it. Don't forget to drain and rinse thoroughly when you get home.

Snapping Turtle Jaw Opener
To get a snapping turtle to let go of something, stick a thin but stiff object up one of its prominent nostrils—a weed stem, thin wire, etc. The turtle is not injured in any way, yet its mouth will pop open.

Race Car Padding Makes Canoe Easy to Carry
Pad the crossbar on a canoe, and it will be much more comfortable to carry on your shoulders when empty and flipped upside down over your head. The closed-cell foam tubing sold in automotive speed shops to pad racing car roll cages is perfect for this and can be secured with black electrical ties. Costs less than $5 and can be installed in 10 minutes.

Use Super Glue to Seal Aluminum Boat Rivets
If an aluminum johnboat starts to take on water, flip it over, let it dry, and then apply a drop of super glue at the base of each rivet. Stops the leaks, and after a year of hard use, still no water in the boat.

Put Fishhooks on a Safety Pin
Keep loose fishing hooks on safety pins, and use a different pin for each size and style of hook. It's a great way to keep a variety handy yet separated.

Disposable Photo Flash Charges Glow Lures
The flash on a cheap disposable camera will light up "glow" fishing lures. They last longer than the film, and while you still

have some unused film in the camera you can use it to take a picture of your catch.

Wide-Mouth Jar Makes a Mini Minnow Bucket
Those wide-mouth clear-plastic jars that hold 2 pounds of peanuts work great to carry live minnows without spilling. Add water and minnows then screw the lid on. Will also keep shotgun shells dry while duck hunting. Mark the shot size on the outside with a felt pen.

Log Safer than Rock for Canoe Ballast
If you are having trouble paddling a canoe by yourself and decide you need a weight in the front for ballast, use a log, not a rock. If the canoe overturns, a rock could cause problems but a log will float, giving you something else to hang onto.

Tip Fish Baits with Black Licorice
Tip baited fishhooks with a small bit from a soft black licorice stick. The scent really attracts fish, and it stays on the hook.

Dress Dry Flies with Outdoor Scotch Guard
Spray dry flies with Outdoor Scotch Guard, let them dry 12 hours and do it again. They will not sink for a long time.

Bait Minnow Traps with Dog Biscuits
Bait minnow traps with dry dog biscuits. Minnows love 'em, and three or four large biscuits broken in half should last 8-10 hours in the water.

Y-Bone Removal for Boneless Walleye Fillets
For bone-free walleye, slice the fillet off the back and side of the fish in the normal way, cut out the rib cage bones and remove the skin. Now pinch the string of Y bones at the tail of the fillet and pull, separating the fillet in half. Now just pull the string of Y bones out of the separated fillet. You get two smaller but boneless fillets.

Rigging Saves Slip Bobbers

To prevent losing a slip bobber when you snag and must break the line, add a second bead and bobber stop to the line between the float and the terminal tackle. If the line breaks down by the hook, this will keep the slip-bobber on the line.

Corn Meal Helps Straighten Rubber Jig Skirts

When rubber jig skirt strands tangle and stick, soak in warm water to relax the strands and then put in a plastic bag with cornmeal and shake. Any remaining tangles should come out, and the cornmeal adds a pleasant if mild scent.

Double-Taper Fly Line Can Fill the Reel Twice

Every four years or so I buy the best double-tapered floating fly line I can afford, and I get 5-weight instead of the 4-weight recommended for my light rod because I want a strong cast with a soft presentation. I cut the 90-foot line in two and put half away, loosely coiled in a sealed bag. Forty-five feet is more than enough with the backing on the reel. After two years, when the line starts to crack, I replace it with the other 45 feet.

Collapse Fishing Jugs for Easier Carry

Gallon milk jugs are great for jug fishing but bulky in the boat. To make them easier to transport, remove the caps and push down on the bottom halves to collapse and deflate; while the jug is still flat, screw the cap back on and it won't re-inflate. Just be sure not to deflate too long before you plan to use them, as this may cause them to distort and not return to shape. When you are ready to fish, unscrew the cap, push the sides back into shape, and screw the cap back on top.

Dental Floss Cutter Handy for Fishing Line, Too

The metal cutter on a dental floss dispenser is also handy for cutting fishing line. Slip the cutter onto the lip of the spool of line you use when making home-snelled hooks and spinners and then secure it in place with a quick-set glue.

Recycle Rubber Worms as Hook Guards

Old chewed-up rubber worms can be cut into 1/2-inch pieces for use as hook guards on other lures. Protects the hook points and also reduces tangling.

Make Your Own Slip Bobbers from Bottle Corks

Turn used bottle corks into slip-bobbers with the tubes that come on cans of spray products like WD-40. Just drill a hole end-to-end through the cork with a 3/64-inch bit and insert the tube.

Toothpick Peg Prevents Plastic Worm Slippage

To prevent a soft plastic worm sliding down the hook and balling up at the bend, push the point of the hook in through the nose of the worm and then slide the head of the worm up the shank past the eye of the hook, so that the hook eye is inside the head of the worm. Now push a 1/4-inch piece of flat toothpick in one side of the worm head, through the eye of the hook, and out the other side of the worm head. Trim excess with a clipper.

Car Undercoating Preserves Nets and Turtle Traps

To ensure long life for turtle traps and fishing nets, spray the netting with rubberized car undercoating after each season. Sold at car parts stores.

Coffee Can Spooling Reduces Fly Line Memory Curl

When you won't be fly-fishing again for a month or more, wrap the first 40 feet of the fly line around a large coffee can instead of taking it up on the smaller fly reel. The larger diameter mitigates the memory curl that tends to form in line stored on a fly reel.

Pipe Cleaner Keeps Rod Sections Together

When packing a two-piece fishing rod, use pipe cleaners to hold the pieces together. The protective fuzz won't scratch the finish, and the stiff wire inside binds the sections securely together.

Salt Leftover Minnows & Freeze for Later

Any live minnows left at the end of the day may be salted and frozen for future use. In fact, when the fish aren't taking live minnows, they sometimes will hit the salted variety.

Look for Bluegill Beds in All the Right Places
Look for bluegill beds offshore from the places with the least human traffic because the panfish are likelier to bed shallow where they won't be disturbed. Also, start the search on the west side of the lake where prevailing wind won't stir up silt and debris. If you can't find any beds in the shallows, look deeper. Bluegills may bed surprisingly deep in clean, clear water.

Petroleum Jelly Keeps Paint Out of Hook Eye
Before painting leadhead jigs or other fishing lures, coat the hook with petroleum jelly. After the paint dries, simply wipe off with a paper towel and the hook will be clean with no paint clogging the eye.

Treat Minnow Water with Hydrogen Peroxide
To keep trapped minnows lively longer, fill the bucket with water from the creek where you trapped them, and then add a capful of hydrogen peroxide to the bucket.

Foil Wrap Hooks and Lures for Safer Carry
To safely leave a fishhook or lure on the line (and avoid tangles, too) wrap it to the rod with heavy-duty aluminum foil. The foil can be reused again and again.

Ice Cleats Work Underwater, Too
To avoid slipping and falling when wading, wear the same ice cleats over your waders that you pull over boots when ice-fishing. They give excellent traction underwater, even on slippery rocks and logs.

Turkey Skin Jig Tippers
The flabby skin around the neck and between the legs of a turkey can be used to tip ice-fishing jigs or spoons. Panfish like the scent, the lively action, and it stays on a hook as well as pork

rind. Can be dyed with food coloring for added eye appeal. It works best raw, so trim it off before roasting the turkey, cut into grub-size pieces, and store in a sealed bag in the freezer.

Bag o' Night Crawlers

When gathering night crawlers for fishing bait, drop them in sandwich-size zipper-type resealable plastic bags. Easy to carry, and for some reason, the crawlers don't try to escape. At the end of the night, just close the bags and pop in the fridge. The next morning, you have chilled but super lively crawlers.

Tied for a Better Hook Set

For sure hook sets, feed the line through from the front of the hook eye instead of from the back before tying it on. Hold the hook by the line and drag it across your thumbnail. You'll instantly feel how much better the front-tied hook bites.

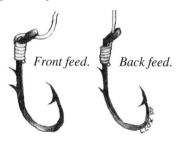

Front feed.   *Back feed.*

Feed line from front of hook eye for better "bite."

Speedometer Cable Makes Great Drift Sinkers

Snag-resistant sinkers for drift-fishing can be made from salvaged speedometer cable (junkyards sell it cheap). Cut 8-inch lengths, bend about 45 degrees in the middle and attach a snap swivel at the bend. Tie a dropper loop or swivel in the main line to attach where needed. Works great when drifting fast water for whitefish or steelhead.

Use the Rod to Measure Fish

To quickly check the length of the fish you catch, mark your rod in 2-inch increments from the reel handle to the first guide. Add different color tapes to mark the legal minimum lengths for different fish.

Crochet Hook Picks Out Bait-Cast Backlash

An inexpensive crochet hook is hard to beat for untangling baitcaster reel backlashes. Size 1 works well and can be found at 'most any sewing shop.

All Bait-Casting Reels Work as Line Counters

To let out the right length of line when trolling with a fully loaded bait-casting reel, pull out the desired length and note the number of handle turns needed to reel the line back up. Because the same applies in reverse, when setting out a trolling pass, you simply drop the lure overboard, turn off the anti-reverse, and count the handle rotations until the same number of turns occurs in reverse.

About-Face for One-Man Canoe Paddling

When alone in a double-ender canoe, sit in the front seat facing the back, and then paddle the canoe stern-first. It will sit level with no ballast needed.

Petroleum Jelly Keeps Rod Tip Ice-Free

To prevent ice buildup on an ice-fishing rod tip, dab on a little petroleum jelly. It sheds water, preventing the ice buildup.

Bait Minnow & Crayfish Traps with Cat Food

To bait minnow and crayfish traps, punch three or four holes in the sides of a cheap can of cat food and place it in the bottom of trap. Draws them much better than soggy bread crumbs.

Gummy Worm a Good Jig Tipper

Colorful, sugar-free gummy worms are great for tipping walleye or bass jigs. Store in a plastic bag with salt, and the gelatin will absorb the salt. A paraffin-like ingredient keeps them from sticking together in the bag and also helps them last in the water.

Make a Leather Thumb Glove for Bait-Casting

To avoid friction burn when "thumbing" a large bait-casting reel, cut the fingers (not the thumb) off an old leather work glove and wear that. Works great when casting heavy weights a long way.

Painting Pole Makes Long-Reach Lure Retriever

Cut the roller off of an extendable ceiling painting pole and bend the remaining shaft into a tight hook. Great for retrieving fishing lures from hard-to-reach snags, especially up in tree branches. Collapsed, it fits easily in a boat locker.

Night Crawlers Over Easy

Leave your worm box upside down. When you need a worm, turn it right-side up, open the lid, and the worms will be on top instead of buried on the bottom.

Grunt Tube Doubles as Fog Horn

My deer grunt tube does double duty as a foghorn on the boat.

Fix Broken Rod Tip with a Paper Clip

For a quick fix of a broken rod tip, open out a paper clip until there is just one bend and two straight legs. Hold the bent end between thumb and finger and bend just that part 90 degrees straight down. Now lay the two legs on either side of the broken rod end, wrap with heavy thread, and super glue it all down tight.

Treble Hook Saves the Liver

When using chicken liver for bait, tie a snap swivel onto the line, push the eye of a No. 4 treble hook through the liver, and then snap the hook to the line. The liver will stay on that three-prong hook much better.

Cast a Wide Net for Grasshoppers

Use a shad cast net to catch grasshoppers for bait. Just throw it over them, same as a school of shad.

Hot Dog Turtle Bait

Use hot dogs for turtle bait. Simply cut to size, impale on hook and twist into place. No muss, no fuss, and turtles love 'em.

Coffee Can & Cement Boat Anchor

A small-boat anchor may be made by setting an old piece of chain in ready-mix cement in one of those plastic coffee containers with the indented handle. Won't bang or scratch the bottom of the boat, and the handle makes it easy to maneuver.

Put Small Tackle in Child-Proof Pill Bottles
Keep small fishing hooks, split shot, etc., in prescription pill bottles with locking child-proof lids that won't accidentally come open and let the contents spill out.

Beef Heart Makes a Good Fishing Bait
Beef heart makes a good fishing bait. Cut a minnow-size strip and impale on a hook. Less hassle than live bait, less expense, and capable of multiple catches without needing to rebait. Just freeze any leftovers and use them on your next outing.

Make a Minnow Bucket from a Milk Jug
Plastic gallon milk jugs are great for carrying live minnows. Cut an opening in the top for easy access but leave the handle on and feed your belt through there for hands-free carry.

Fresh Bread Restores Marshmallow Baits
To refresh dried-out marshmallow baits left over from the last fishing trip, put a slice of fresh bread in a plastic bag with the marshmallows, seal tight, and 12 hours later, they're back as good as new.

Thread Wrap Keeps Chicken Liver on Hook
When using chicken liver for fishing bait, wrap it with thread and it won't fly off the hook when you cast. Break off 18 inches and lay it across a rock. Hook the liver the way you like, lay it on the thread and wrap the entire piece finishing with two snug wraps. No need to tie the thread. The liver won't come off when you cast.

Tic-Tac Handy Bait Dispenser
Instead of putting up with the lid constantly falling off of the cheap plastic containers the bait shops use for mealworms, put

them in a Tic Tac dispenser. Fits easily in a pocket, and you can shake out one at a time as needed.

Easy-Add Eyelet for Tying Tippet to Fly Line
For an eyelet for tying tippet to fly line, cut the curve and point off a No. 10 fishhook and insert just the shank into the fly line with a little super glue. Works fine with most level lines.

Trap Bait Leeches with a Coffee Can
To trap leeches for fishing bait, take the plastic lid off a metal coffee can and cut a half-dozen V-shaped slits in it, leaving the flaps connected but pushed in a little. Put meat in the can, snap the lid back on and place the can in a stream or pond with leeches. The leeches slide in through the slits yet can't seem to find their way back out.

Two-Lure Tandem Trolling Rig
To make a tandem trolling rig, remove the back treble hook from a deep-diving crankbait and attach an in-line spinner with 30 inches of monofilament. With 12 inches of connecting line, may be used for casting and reeling.

Build a Better Two-Door Worm Box
Build a two-door worm box from 3/4-inch plywood 24 inches long, 24 inches wide, and 5 inches deep. Attach the top and bottom panels with door hinges on one side and screen door hooks on the other to hold them tight. Fill with "woodsy" topsoil and night crawlers. Then, when you want a worm, turn the box over before opening and the worms will always be on top.

PVC Pipe Turtle Trap Floats
Turtle traps must be set with a couple inches of trap above the waterline so trapped turtles don't drown. Address this with floats made of sturdy yet light 4-inch PVC pipe and end caps. Measure the length of the trap and cut two pieces of pipe to fit. Glue caps on both ends of both pipes. Attach to the trap with wire ties or heavy nylon cord.

Tangle-Free Tip-Up Transport

To keep ice-fishing tip-ups from tangling, cut 12-inch sections of 4-inch PVC pipe and fasten them to the inside of a 5-gallon bucket with sheet-metal screws. One fully-rigged tip-up fits snugly in each section.

Boat Battery Box Shoulder Strap

To make it easier to carry a portable trolling motor battery, cut two parallel slots in either end of the plastic battery box and thread 2-inch nylon strapping through the slots in such a way that the strap goes in through the slots on one side, under the box, and then back up and out the slots on the other side. Attach a nylon plastic parachute buckle on the strap ends. The webbing is wide enough to comfortably distribute the load on a shoulder. When carrying, be sure to put the lid back on the battery box to contain acid spills.

Jug Fishing Made Easy

One-quart plastic bleach bottles can be rigged for jug fishing with braided line cut to length, hook and optional sinker attached. A "rubber band" cut 1/2-inch wide from a bicycle inner tube holds line and hook safely in place without tangles; reflective tape (optional) makes the white bottle even more visible at night. Name and address can be written on the bottom with a waterproof marker. Empties may be found in the dumpster outside any laundromat.

Make Your Own Ice Safety Spikes

Make safety spikes for ice-fishing and trapping on ice by cutting wood handles and then pressing heavy gauge galvanized nails into the ends. Cut and sand so they are easy to grip, and add a neck lanyard for easy carry with instant access.

Make Flutter Spoons from Trap Tags

Copper trap tags are great for "tagging" fish, too. Just put an O-ring through the hole and punch or drill another hole near the opposite end. Add a No. 6 hook and tip with a minnow. You can bend it to get different actions, and the copper mimics a mud minnow. Smallmouth bass really go for them, and they are great for jumbo perch, too.

Bleach Bottle Makes a Great Boat Bailing Bucket

Cut the bottom off of a bleach bottle, put the cap back on, and it makes a great flexible bailing bucket for the boat. Remove the cap and it also serves as a funnel. Put a wheel balancing weight inside the handle, and it won't blow out of the boat as easily.

Easy Fishing Line Weed Guard

To keep little bits of floating weed and other debris from fouling fishing lures when they slide down the line, each time you change lures, just leave the old knot and an inch or so of line on the lure eye. Over time, it will look like a spider and catch weeds before they foul the lure.

Pipe Cleaner Paint Brush for Jigheads

Dipping jig heads in paint plugs the hook eyes. Instead, just paint them with a pipe cleaner. Also ideal for applying epoxy coatings. After a pipe cleaner is used, just clip off the end and throw that part away. Trimmed this way after each use, a pipe cleaner may be reused many times.

Rod Holder in a Bucket

I made a rod holder for fishing off piers or rocky shorelines from an old 5-gallon pail and a PVC 1-1/2-inch plumber's tee with screw-in clean-out. Use a screw to mark and then cut out a hole under the rim of the pail and screw tee into hole. Use the bucket to carry in gear, and when you are ready to fish, empty the bucket, add water for weight and insert the rod handle in the tee. With a rope on the bucket handle, you can even lower it off docks and sea walls. Works like a charm.

Ice-Free Slip Bobber

To prevent a plastic slip bobber freezing to the line while ice-fishing, straighten out a paper clip, heat it with a lighter, and push it through the bottom of the slip tube, the part that stays underwater when in use. Run the line through this hole, and the line and the stop knot both are always underwater where they won't freeze.

Fisherman's Key Ring

A nifty key ring (and Christmas gift for the angler) can be made by removing the hooks from a fishing lure and attaching a key ring to the tail end. Use a small lure, as a large lure will be too bulky to carry in a pocket.

Handy Milk Carton Boat Bailer

A handy boat bail can be made from an empty plastic milk jug. With knife or scissors, cut off the top of the carton, retaining the handle side. It's flexible enough to "scoop" water up from an uneven floor.

Cool Bait Bucket

To keep bait fresh, insulate your minnow bucket with foam rubber cut from old furniture cushions. You also need a milk crate and an electric carving knife (the only thing that nicely cuts foam rubber.) Cut layers of foam rubber that fit snugly in the crate and then cut a bucket size hole out of the middle of each layer. Put the foam in the crate, the bucket in the foam, and then dampen the foam to keep bait cooler. Also makes the bucket less likely to tip over.

Hearty Catfish Baits

Save chicken and turkey hearts for catfish baits. Bloody and smelly like liver, but unlike liver, tough on the hook. I frequently catch more than one catfish on the same chunk. Store in the freezer, in resealable plastic bags.

Camping & Hiking

Solar Lawn Lights for Camping

Solar-powered lawn lights are great around a
family campsite. Place them during the day and let the
sun charge them. They come on automatically at dusk,
and everyone will be able to safely see their way around
the site. At bedtime, let the children take one into the tent
for a night light. No lantern to accidentally kick over,
and no worry about the batteries running down
when they fall asleep and leave it on.

Cans Hold Grate and Hot Water for the Dishes

Fill three of those big No. 10 tin cans with water and use them to support the grill over a campfire. At meal's end, you will have gallons of water ready and waiting to do the dishes.

Panty Hose Soap Holder

Cut the leg from an old pair of panty hose, put a bar of soap in it, and tie it off by the water. You now have soap and a lightly abrasive scrubber for washing hands.

Salted Ice Freezes Colder and Lasts Longer

Put 1/2-cup of salt in a gallon jug of water, freeze it, and the ice will be colder and last longer than plain frozen water.

Dumb-as-a-Fox Knife Sharpening Tip

Before you go to camp with buddies, remember *not* to sharpen your knives. Just take them along. My buddies invariably bring all kinds of stones and oils. By the end of the first day, after they have honed all of their knives and everything else (including the tent stakes) to razor sharpness, I say something like, "Gee, guys, I forgot my Arkansas stone." Then I dump my rucksack of knives on a sleeping bag and watch them fight over them.

Camp Kitchen Skillet Clean Up

To clean a skillet when camping, leave in some grease, throw in a couple of double handfuls of campfire ashes, add a half-cup of water, stir and leave overnight. The ashes leach out potassium hydroxide, which produces soap. The next morning, a little washing does the trick.

Fill Camping Lanterns Without Overflow

Camping lanterns often overflow during fueling, even when using a funnel. To prevent this, cut the top half off of a dishwashing liquid bottle with a pull-top spout and use this for a funnel. The instant the lantern is full, simply push down and the spout closes. Any fuel still in the funnel can be easily returned to the fuel can.

Fast Food, Indeed

For a hot, fast meal in the field, place a few hot dogs in a wide-mouth thermos and fill the rest of the way with boiling hot water. A couple of buns and ketchup packets are all you need.

Preheated Hot Vacuum Bottles Last Longer

To keep food or drink hot longer, preheat the vacuum bottle by putting hot water in it while you are preparing the food. When it is ready, pour out the water and refill the bottle with the food.

Gas Lantern Doubles as Hand Warmer

Gas lanterns can also warm your hands, and they work even better if you cut an 8-inch slit 6 inches up from the bottom of each narrow side of a paper grocery bag, slip your hands through these openings and hold the bag open over the lantern.

DIY Lantern Light Reflector

A reflector for a Coleman-type gas lantern can be made from a No. 10 vegetable can. First, use a triangular can opener to punch ventilation holes around the perimeter of the can bottom (the top, of course, has been removed). Next, use tin snips to cut out one side of the can, leaving the bottom intact and attached to the remaining sides. Drill a hole in the center of the bottom of the can, remove the nut that holds the lantern top, install the reflector and replace the nut. For more or less light, cut more or less out of the can wall. Beware that the reflector will get hot.

Use Freezer Bags for Lightweight Water Bags

When backpacking, bring a couple of gallon-size zipper-type resealable food storage bags. Use your filter/purifier to treat available water and then fill the bags for carry. The freezer-grade bags are lightweight yet very leak resistant.

Compact Camp Stove in a Can

Store your backpack stove in a large coffee can with a snap-on lid. Wrap the stove in an old towel to keep it from getting banged up and to absorb any leaked fuel. The can also may be used as a pot for boiling water; when it gets rusty, simply replace.

Make Your Own Alcohol Hand Cleaner

Mix 2 cups rubbing alcohol with 1 cup water and 1/2-teaspoon dish soap to make a hand cleaner that works well where regular soap and water are not handy. Store in an old squirt-top bottle. The soap and water clean while the alcohol kills germs. Then it evaporates equally, leaving virtually no residue on your hands.

Pin Car Keys in Your Pocket to Prevent Loss

Before entering the woods, put your car keys on a large key ring, put the ring in your pocket, and then pass a safety pin through the ring and the pocket. Close the safety pin to avoid the sinking feeling that comes when you put your hand in an empty pocket that used to hold your keys.

Primitive Camp Shower

For a camp shower anywhere, drill three holes in the side near the bottom of an empty bleach jug, tie 8 feet of rope to the handle, drill a hole through a bar of soap and tie that to the other end of the rope. Cover the jug holes with duct tape, fill the jug with hot water, put the cap back on, and toss the soap (with attached rope) over a tree limb a couple of feet above head high. Let the soap and rope wrap around the limb three times and the jug should hold at the desired height. When you are ready to shower, pull the tape. To make the water flow faster, loosen the lid on the jug. Rig up two and you can suds with one, rinse with the other.

Tin Can Campfire Potato Baker

If you want to bake a potato in camp, put it in an empty tin can and bury it to the brim in hot campfire coals. The potato cooks up nicely and comes out clean.

Simple Solar-Heated Camp Shower

A simple solar-heated camp shower may be made by simply filling a black garbage bag with water and leaving it out in the sun. Use one of the heavy grade bags, and check for leaks. When you are ready for a shower, hang it from a tree and punch a few holes in the bottom, sort of like a big pepper shaker.

Freeze Milk for the Camping Cooler
Freeze a gallon of milk and put it in your cooler like a block of ice. Helps keep the rest of the food cold, and as it thaws, you get cold milk.

Freeze the Whole Cooler for Ice that Lasts
Instead of adding ice to a small cooler, fill the cooler itself about half full of water and freeze the whole thing.

Sleep Cheap on a Carpet Pad
Instead of buying an expensive self-inflating mat for under your sleeping bag, use a piece of foam carpet pad. It rolls up nicely and costs about $2 at a carpet store.

Keep Sleeping Bag in a 5-Gallon Bucket
A 5-gallon bucket with a watertight lid is ideal for stowing a sleeping bag. Most fit nicely with a pillow and stay dry even in the back of an open pickup.

Always Handy Lantern Mantles
Duct tape replacement mantles for gas lanterns, package and all, in the hollow at the bottom of the base of the lantern. You always have replacement mantles on hand.

Turn Flashlight Batteries to Boost Brightness
When a flashlight goes dim, take out the batteries and put the one that was in the back in the front and the one that was in the front in the back. The light will brighten long enough to hopefully get you back to camp.

Pliers a Quick Fix for Failing Tent Zipper
If the opening on a tent pulls open after you zipper it shut, try using pliers to carefully pinch the zipper sides a little closer

together. This simple trick is worth a try when any light zipper starts opening behind the closer.

A Plan to Extend the Ice Age

To get another couple of days out of a large camp cooler, fold an old rug so it fits the bottom, dampen, freeze, and put in the cooler. Now lay four milk jugs of frozen water on the rug and pack the frozen food around the jugs. Layer newspaper on top of the frozen goods and then put in the milk, bacon, etc. A final thick layer of newspaper goes on top. Close and latch the lid, cover with a blanket or sleeping bag, and keep it in the shade.

Coat Pot with Dish Soap for Easier Clean Up

Before cooking over a campfire or stove, lightly coat the bottoms of skillets, pots and pans with liquid dishwashing soap and let it dry. To clean, rinse with water and the soot melts away.

Rub Fire Grate with Potato to Save Fish Fillets

Before grilling fish in camp, cut a potato crossways and rub the surface of the grill with the cut side. Prevents the delicate fillets sticking to a hot, dry grill.

Glow in the Dark Cooler Light

Put kids' glow-sticks in the cooler. When you open the lid at night, it's like a refrigerator light coming on, and a stick lasts three or four days when kept cool that way.

Power Crank for Pop-Up Camper

When you get tired of hand-cranking to lift a pop-up truck camper, cut a groove in the end of a 9/16-inch-deep well socket to match the slot where the hand crank fits. A 1/4-inch adapter attaches the socket to a cordless power drill. Now, just pull the trigger and watch the top go up.

2-Liter Bottles Make Handy Cooler Ice

Clean 2-liter pop bottles, fill with water and freeze for the camping cooler. The solid ice lasts longer than crushed, and as it melts, the water stays in the bottle so it doesn't make a mess in the cooler. Also stays clean for drinking or other purposes.

Pocket Fuel for Backpack Cooking
Trioxane fuel bars (inexpensive at Army surplus stores) come in foil pouches that easily fit in a shirt pocket. They start with just a spark and then burn hot enough and long enough to boil water.

Firewood-Splitting Hand Axe
To prevent an Estwing axe getting stuck while splitting firewood, grind both sides of the inside point of the chopping edge and head a little thinner than the outside point.

Grind shaded area.

Aluminum Foil Campfire Oven
You can make a reflector oven for baking biscuits, etc., with a campfire from nothing more than heavy duty aluminum foil and three sticks. Cut a pair of forked sticks about 2 feet long and drive them in the ground about 2 feet apart, right beside the campfire. Lay a cross stick in the two forks, wrap aluminum foil around this top stick three or four times to secure, and then stretch it down to the ground, following the support sticks. Secure at the bottom with a small log laid crossways and close the sides with additional foil.

Instant Running Water from a Jug
For washing hands where there is no running water, drill a 3/16-inch hole in the lid of an empty gallon milk jug. When you fill the jug with water, put the cap on and tip the jug on its side, you get a small but steady stream of running water.

Warm a Sleeping Bag with Car Engine Heat
When I stop at a campsite for a quick overnight stay, I open my sleeping bag and spread it over the hood of the car while I pitch the tent. When the tent's up, I zip the sleeping bag closed,

trapping the warmth from the car engine inside.

Sleeping Bag Extends Cooler Ice Time
Slide a camp cooler into an old insulated sleeping bag and the ice will keep for an extra day or two.

Cedar Shim Fire Starter
For an easy fire starter, pick up a package of the cedar shims that carpenters use. They are inexpensive at building supply stores, lightweight, come wrapped in weatherproof plastic and tapered for easy lighting.

Denture Cleanser Good for Water Bottles, Too
To cleanse the funky smell out of a used water bottle, fill with water, drop in a denture-cleansing tablet, and let soak overnight. Also kills any bacteria.

Hand Warmers Also Warm Sleeping Bags
If your feet get cold when camping in the winter, toss a chemical hand warmer in the bottom of your sleeping bag. Good ones last 8 to 10 hours and cost less than a buck each. If you wake up with cold toes, just shake the warmer and it heats back up. Lets you use a lighter bag on backpack hunts.

Nail Apron Makes a Handy Cot Organizer
A carpenter's nail apron makes a handy camping cot organizer— great for keeping eyeglasses, flashlight, etc., up off the ground, safe and handy. Just tie the apron strings to the end and middle support of the cot.

Put Long Johns in Sleeping Bag for Warmer Wake Up
To make the morning wake-up more comfortable, sleep with dry long johns at the bottom of your sleeping bag and pull them on before climbing out. Also helps keep feet warm during the night.

Milk Cartons Great for Packing Gear
Cardboard milk cartons are ideal for packing the small stuff in

a camp kit. Clean, fill with gear, fold over the top and duct tape shut to make dry and spill-proof. Can be molded to fit a pack, and cut strips of the waxed carton make great fire starters.

Plywood Campfire Windbreak
Make a free-standing campfire windbreak from two 48-by-30-inch sheets of plywood hinged together lengthwise. Open it no further than the point it still forms an angle, and it will stand in all but the strongest wind. Aluminum flashing on the inside increases heat-reflection. Easy to fold and carry.

Pine Bough Ground Bed
To make a soft and level bed on the ground, place pine boughs in parallel overlapping lines with the cut ends on the outside. Now lay a sleeping bag on top.

Nail a Faster Campfire Baked Potato
Before wrapping a potato in foil and tossing it into the coals of a campfire, insert an ordinary 16-penny steel nail into the center of the potato. Cuts the baking time nearly in half.

The Original Scouring Pad
To remove the soot that gets on a pan when cooking over a campfire, dip a charcoal-burnt stick in water and scrub with it like a scouring pad. Works great and keeps the "black" off your other cleaning gear.

Lid on Bottom Keeps Lantern Mantles Handy
The snap lid from a 2-pound coffee can fits snugly on the bottom of most two-mantle Coleman lanterns with just enough dry space between the two to hold two packs of mantles and a pack of matches. Secure with a wrap of duct tape.

Inflate Plastic Bag for Ultra Light Camping Pillow
Make an ultra light camping pillow with two gallon-size zipper-close freezer bags. Inflate one bag half full of air, place it inside the other bag, and then fully inflate the outside bag by sealing all

but a small opening in the corner and blowing in that opening. A straw may be helpful, but not necessary.

Plastic-Wrap Sleeping Bag to Stay Warm in Winter
Wrap your sleeping bag with heavy-duty Visqueen construction plastic to stay warmer in winter. Folds up to easily fit in a pack.

Coffee Filter Extends Costly Water Filter Life
Twist-tie a paper coffee filter to the intake end of a backpacking water filter. It acts as a pre-filter to increase the life of the water filter's much more expensive internal filter.

Charcoal Briquettes Absorb Cooler Odors
To get odors out of a cooler, drop in five or six charcoal briquettes (same ones that are sold for barbecuing) and close the top. Most odors are absorbed overnight.

Take a Wok in the Woods for Camp Cooking
A Chinese steel wok makes a versatile camp cooking utensil. Ideal for frying over a campfire, and the large surface heats water quickly to a rapid boil for pasta or to do the dishes afterwards.

Use Water to Free Stuck Stakes
To pull a stubborn tent stake, pour a little water around the shaft and tap it. Repeat until the stake pulls. Works with plastic or metal, and a single two-liter pop bottle holds enough water to pull 30 tough stakes.

Break Eggs Before Packing Them
Instead of trying to pack unbroken eggs into a campsite, break them into a narrow plastic jar with a lid. No mess, and they naturally pour back out one at a time.

Simple Sun-Powered Water Heating
To heat water at camp, paint 5-gallon plastic buckets and lids flat black. Fill with water and set in the sun during the day. The sun heats the water more than you might imagine. In the evening, cover with blankets to hold in that heat.

Wilderness Living
&
Emergency Survival

*Road flares are great
signalling devices day or night
and also make dependable
fire starters.*

Road Flare Also a Dependable Fire Starter

A road flare should be in everyone's emergency
kit. They work as signalling devices day or night and also
make super-dependable fire starters. Most are waterproof
and have a built-in striker. All light and then stay lit even
in blowing rain; burns hot enough and long enough
to dry out and ignite damp kindling.

Decoy Cord Better, Cheaper than Parachute Cord

Survivalists often advise carrying a little parachute cord for emergencies, but braided nylon decoy cord can be equally strong, less expensive and less bulky. It comes in handy for bootlaces, lanyards, tie-downs and countless other everyday uses, too. Melt the cut ends of the cord to prevent unraveling.

A Hairy Way to Dry Damp Matches

When damp (not wet) matches won't strike, rub them lightly in your hair or beard one at a time until they are dry enough to ignite (doesn't take long). Wooden "farmer" matches work best, but if the matches are of the book type, it helps to also rub the sandpaper striking surface.

File Does Double Duty in Fire-Starting Kit

If you keep a magnesium fire starter in your survival kit, a good way to shave the magnesium off is with a piece of old file. You won't dull your knife, and you can also strike the sparking insert with the file.

Cotton Ball & Petroleum Jelly Rainy Day Tinder

Roll cotton balls in petroleum jelly and store in a sealed container (35mm film canisters work great, if you can find them). Before you try to light a fire, place two or three in with the tinder. They burn long enough to get a fire going even on a damp day.

Freeze-Proof Winter Storage for Canned Goods

In winter in an unheated cabin, canned goods often freeze. Instead, cut a hole in lake ice, put the cans in a bran sack, and submerge below ice level. They will not freeze; but use a permanent marker to mark the contents on the top of each can, because the labels may soak off.

Revive Cold-Numbed Fingers and Toes

If you lose the feeling in your fingers in numbing cold, and there is no other heat source, wrap your arms around your torso, let your wrists go limp, and then swing your arms and let your hands slap against your back and sides. After 20 times, let your arms hang straight down at your sides. Repeat until the feeling returns. As for your toes, stomp as hard as you can as long as you can. Then hang your feet over a log and let the blood flow. Both techniques work by forcing warmer blood into cold extremities. The stinging you feel is actually a sign that it is working.

Handy Sling for Packing Snowshoes

I carry an inexpensive nylon rifle sling with a loop on one end and a snap hook on the other. When the trail gets too rough for snowshoes, I loop the sling through the snowshoes and throw them over my shoulder for easier carry.

Red Lens No Good with Topo Maps

Never use a red-lensed light to read a USGS topo map at night. It makes the red ink invisible, unintentionally hiding much of the information. The military uses a red/brown map ink to enable troops to still read them with red filters on their flashlights.

Carry WD-40 on Your Four-Wheeler

When four-wheeling in the backcountry, always carry WD-40 with your tools. When big mud holes get the distributor wet and stall out the motor, simply take off the distributor cap and spray a little WD-40 in there. It displaces the water, allowing the vehicle to start and run again.

Wet-Weather Tinder

If you need to build an emergency fire but everything is wet, look for an old shagbark hickory. The trunk should have many layers of bark, and the layers underneath should be dry.

Use Flashlight Battery to Spark a Fire

Fill a small canister (35mm film canisters are ideal, if you can find them) with 4/0 steel wool, close the lid and place in a bag with a flashlight battery. If you run out of matches or they become wet, the steel wool can be used to start a fire. Roll up a piece into a "rope" and touch each end to the battery terminals.

If the battery isn't strong enough, use two batteries in series. The steel wool also makes great tinder.

Turn Snow-Go Before Stopping in Deep Snow

Before you stop a snowmachine in deep snow, always make a U-turn then stop on your own packed track. This helps prevent the machine sinking when you accelerate to leave. And carry a pair of snowshoes—just in case.

Clothespin Clip-on Trail Markers

Spray-paint spring-type clothespins blaze orange, or staple on small pieces of surveyor's tape and put them in your pack to use as trail markers. They can be clipped on brush quickly and just as easily removed to be reused over again.

Alcohol Swabs Double as Fire Starters

The sealed alcohol swabs sold at the drugstore make great fire starters. Just drop a handful in your pack.

Find South with a Watch Face

If you lose your bearings, an analog watch (the type with hands) can help you find south. Turn the watch until the hour hand points at the sun. The spot on the dial halfway between the hour hand and the number 12 should face south.

Dryer Lint Fire Starter

Save the lint from a clothes dryer screen, roll it into golf ball-size lumps and put in a zip-type resealable plastic bag. Lint ignites promptly then burns long and hot enough to start even damp kindling. A little goes a long way.

Lube Ski-Doo with Liquid Dish Soap

When running a Ski-Doo on hard-packed trails or glare ice where there isn't enough loose snow, lube the slider with liquid dish soap. A few squirts should get you a couple of miles before it starts to heat up again.

Surefire Wet Weather Matches

Lay a dozen wooden strike-anywhere matches 1/4-inch apart. Glue sewing thread to the ends of the matches. Dip in melted paraffin and hang until wax hardens.

Fiberglass Protects Snowshoes

Apply fiberglass to snowshoes and they will last longer. Even if the webbing gets cut, it does not fray and unravel as easily.

Milk Carton Fire Starters

Simply cut a waxed cardboard milk carton into strips and pack as a lightweight fire starter. Waxed cardboard lights even when damp and burns hot for a surprisingly long time.

Easy-on Easy-Off Inner Tube Snowshoe Bindings

The slickest snowshoe binding is just a simple toe strap and elastic band around the boot, with a pull tab on the back. Pull on over the boot. If you fall, hold the tab down and pull your foot up and out. Can be cut out of an old truck inner tube, and a spare may be carried in a pocket in case one breaks.

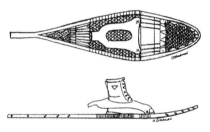

Easy-on easy-off binding.

Emery Cloth Match Striker

Carry a piece of 120-grit emery cloth in your wallet for those strike-anywhere matches that don't want to strike anywhere. Also, it can touch up a knife edge, hook point or whatever when a stone isn't handy.

Fire in the Buttstock Hole

Place strike-anywhere matches and a strip of emery cloth in a sealed plastic bag, roll it up and stick it in the hole behind the butt plate of a gun's stock. It will always be there in an emergency.

Sheep Wool Keeps Fingers Warm

To keep fingers warmer, put a little plug of sheep wool into each fingertip of your winter gloves.

Start Windy Day Fire in a Paper Bag

To start a fire on a windy day, puff up a paper lunch sack, put dry tinder in the bag and light it. The bag blocks the wind long enough for the tinder to get going and then light the bag.

Open Your Mouth and Your Ears

Old-time woodsmen knew to open their mouths slightly to better hear distant sounds. Ears and throat are connected by the eustachian tube or canal. Just as sound waves enter your ears, they will also enter your open mouth to improve hearing.

Serrated Edge Can Be a Life Saver

For emergencies, carry a knife with at least a partially serrated blade. A serrated edge cuts things like wet rope and other tough materials much more quickly than does a straight-edge blade.

Charcoal Briquette Fire Starter

Put four of the charcoal briquettes that already have lighting fluid in them in a sealed plastic bag. With the touch of a match, you get a small but instant fire that lasts a long time. Add sticks to build a bigger blaze.

Teflon Pads Better for Sleds

Remove the steel shoes from a snow sled and replace with Teflon—the kind used on hockey rink sides. It is lightweight, tough enough to last, and slides much easier than steel.

Pine Knot Fire Starters

To start a fire on a wet day, dig in the heap of debris that accumulates around an old rotting pine tree and you may find lumps of hardened wood. These pine knots are preserved because they contain lots of resinous pitch, which also makes them easy to light and long-lasting fire starters.

Pack Dental Floss in Emergency Kit

Every outdoor emergency kit should include at least a couple of spools of dental floss. It is compact, strong, and can be used for everything from fishing line to sewing up a wound. Braid several strands together and make a short rope. The floss holder provides an easy way to cut the amount you need.

Backwoods Bumper Hitch Porta Potty

If you have a trailer hitch on your vehicle's bumper, you can make a go-anywhere toilet by simply bolting a toilet seat to a spare trailer hitch ball mount. Easy to install and remove.

Ice-Proof Snowshoes with Electric Tape

Wrap wood snowshoe tails, the webbing under the instep, and all leading edges around the frame with electrical tape. Ice will not collect on the tape regardless of conditions.

Boot Lace Handy for Emergency Snowshoe Fix

Tie an old leather boot lace to the front of a snowshoe and it will be there for emergency repair of webbing or binding.

Emergency Whistles for Kids

Before taking youngsters out in the woods, hang loud whistles around their necks and teach them to blow three loud bursts if they are lost or otherwise need help. But stress that the whistles are not toys and should only be blown when help is needed.

Gun Stock Survival Kit

Pull the butt plate from a rifle stock and drill a hole into the wood the same diameter as the cartridge the gun shoots then slide in some extras. As for the hole that's already there, make it big enough to hold a lighter and other compact survival items in a sealed plastic bag. When done, just screw the butt plate back on.

Masking Tape a Fire Starter, Too

A roll of lightweight masking tape serves many purposes in an emergency kit, good for everything from closing a wound to starting a fire. Inner layers on the roll stay dry even in damp weather. Peel off about 20 inches, ball it up like newspaper, and it will burn long and hot.

Wind-Up Flashlight Most Dependable

Put a wind-up flashlight in your pack. They don't put out that much light, but they don't need sunlight like solar lights, and they don't have batteries that can go dead, either.

Eyeglasses for Emergency Fire Starting

If you are caught in a survival situation with nothing better, you may be able to start a fire with your eyeglasses. Use the lenses to focus the rays of the sun on dry tinder. It may take a while, but if the lenses are strong enough, it will work.

CD Signaling Mirror

An old CD makes a good emergency signaling mirror. They are super reflective with a center hole already cut for viewing and aiming the light.

Vacuum Pack Your Survival Kit

Use one of those vacuum packing plastic-bag sealers (sold for freezing food) to bundle emergency items into a single compact package. Keeps things like wood matches, socks, space blankets, toilet paper, etc., dry and ready to go when needed.

Clean Wounds and Start a Fire

Alcohol-based gel hand sanitizers are good for cleaning burns and scrapes and may even help get a fire going on a wet day. Squirt a little on the kindling before you light it. The small personal-size bottles are ideal for a compact kit.

Solar Lawn Lights Good for Emergencies

Place solar lawn lights around your house, and if you ever lose electric power, you can simply bring some inside to provide emergency lighting with no fire risk.

Rural Living

The Adirondack Mousetrap

To trap mice in numbers, make an Adirondack Mousetrap from a 5-gallon plastic bucket, a plastic pop bottle, and a wire coat hanger. Straighten the hanger and cut a length 4 inches longer than the width of the bucket. Heat one end and use it to melt holes in opposite sides of the bucket, 2 inches down from the top. Now use the wire to melt a hole in the center of the pop bottle bottom and also in the plastic cap. Insert wire lengthwise through the holes in bucket and bottle, and bend the ends to secure all loosely in place. Pour a gallon of water in the bucket, smear peanut butter on the pop bottle, and provide a ramp for mice to climb up to the lip of the bucket. When a mouse walks out on the bottle for the peanut butter, the bottle will spin and dump the mouse in the water, where it will drown.

Mobile Home Anchors for Off-Road Winching

Carry two mobile home anchors and a 4-foot section of sturdy steel pipe in your off-road vehicle. Then, when you get stuck where there is nothing to attach a chain to, you may still winch yourself free. Use the pipe to screw the anchors into the ground. Position the anchors a couple of feet apart, angled a bit toward each other but still straight enough to slip the pipe through both of the anchor eyelets. After turning the anchors deeply into the earth, slip the pipe through the eyelets and attach a chain. Use your handyman jack to winch out, but watch those anchors closely as they may pull loose.

Handy Fire Starter for Fireplace or Wood Stove

Make fire starters by mixing sawdust (hardwood, the coarser the better) with melted paraffin. Use a broom handle to press the cooling mixture into the cardboard tube left over from a roll of paper towel. After it hardens, cut the "log" into 1-1/2-inch pieces and wrap in aluminum foil. To start a fire, unwrap a piece, dish out one end with a knife, and then light the cardboard with a match. Burns for about 10 minutes, hot enough and long enough to ignite even damp kindling, and is totally waterproof.

Render Beaver Fat into Waterproof Oil

As you cut the fat from beavers store in a large coffee can in the freezer until the can is three-quarters full. Allow to thaw and then heat to a low boil on a fire or stove (preferably outdoors). Let cool, somewhat, and then pour the oil off the top into a clean glass container, filtering out any solids. The oil should look like light maple syrup and will last for years when sealed. Works well as a leather preservative and to improve water repellency. The fat from bears and coons may work equally well.

Replaceable Razor Blade Knife Always Sharp

For all-round practicality, nothing beats a replaceable razor-blade knife, or drywall knife, as some call them. The throw-away type with blades that just snap off cost about a dollar, and by simply snapping off the end section when it gets dull, you have a razor-sharp edge. I use mine for everything from whittling tinder to skinning deer.

S-Hooks for Crossing Barbed Wire Fence
To cross a high barbed wire fence, carry a couple of stout S-hooks. Halfway between two posts, pull the top wires together and use a hook to hold them together. Pull the bottom wires together and use the other hook to hold these together. Now step through the gap in the middle. It won't damage the fence, and you won't snag your clothing.

Dry Ginseng Faster with a Food Dehydrator
Use a food dehydrator with a fan to dry ginseng. Put roots of the same size on the same tray, and when each tray is done it can be removed and the larger roots left to continue drying. Time for drying varies, but it will be hours instead of days.

Overnight Leather Boot Drying
Fill a damp leather boot with oil-absorbing sweeping compound (sold at auto parts stores). Dump out in the morning, and the boot will be dry. After the compound dries, you can use it again.

Super Glue a Super Fast Wader Patch
Use super glue to patch small leaks in waders, rubber boots, etc. Works great and dries in seconds.

A Faster Way to Dry Wet Boots
To dry wet boots in a hurry, heat newspaper in the oven (be sure the paper does not touch the heating element) and stuff it in the boots. Remove when damp and replace with hot, dry newspaper every 10 minutes or so, and the boots will dry in no time.

Vegetable Oil Pine Resin Remover
Laundry detergent does not remove pine tree resin. Instead, rub vegetable oil into the stains. This quickly dissolves the resin into an oily layer, which then easily washes out with soap and water. Works the same if you get resin or tar on your hands. If you have

no vegetable oil, butter will do.

Cleaning Ceramic Sharpening Sticks
When ceramic sharpening sticks become dark and clogged with metal shavings, renew them by scrubbing with Comet or Ajax cleanser. After rinsing, the ceramic looks and sharpens like new.

Put a Spare Bulb in the Flashlight
Wrap a spare flashlight bulb in soft cloth and store it inside the flashlight battery compartment. Most have plenty enough space either behind the reflector or in the back under the spring.

Leave the Leaves on to Dry Firewood Faster
Leave the green tops on trees that are cut for firewood or poles. As the foliage dries, it will draw much of the moisture from the trunk wood. Then just trim away.

Newspaper Burn Gets Chimney Going
Wood stoves can be hard to light when damp air hangs in the chimney. The solution is to light a ball of newspaper and place it inside near the opening of the stovepipe. This drives out the heavy air, and the chimney will draft when the fire is lit.

Avoid Chain Saw Oil Can Overflow
The next time you open a gallon can of chain saw oil, poke a small round hole in the aluminum seal instead of removing it. Then the flow of oil won't come out bigger than the hole in the chain saw. Tear off the whole seal and the flow of oil will overwhelm the smaller hole in the chain saw.

PVC Pipe & Pop Bottle Yellow Jacket Trap
A yellow jacket trap can be made from a 2-liter plastic soda bottle and a 10-inch length of 1-inch PVC pipe. Cut angled ends on the pipe; then cut a hole in the bottom center of the pipe. Insert the pipe through the bottle. Next, fill the bottle half full with water and drop a small piece of waste fish meat in. Put the cap back on the bottle. A little sugar sprinkled on the pipe ends

helps to encourage yellow jackets to crawl in, and once they are inside, they do not crawl back out. Hang the trap with heavy twine in areas of high concentrations of the winged pests.

Shower Curtain Rod Secures Gear in Truck Bed
A telescoping twist-type shower curtain rod can be used to secure gear in the bed of a pickup truck. They are reasonably cheap, durable, impervious to water damage and designed not to slip.

Heavy Metal Mouse Stoppers
To keep mice out of the house, stuff aluminum foil or steel wool into any cracks or holes that the mice might be using. The metal hurts their mouths, and they don't chew through it.

Use Duct Tape to Keep Socks Up
To stop socks working down in boots or waders, pull the socks up, the pants legs down, and then tape the legs to the socks with duct tape. Wear them all day and they won't slip.

Basic Bucket Mousetrap
To keep mice under control, I spread peanut butter in the bottom of a 6-gallon plastic bucket and set the bucket against a wall the mice can climb. They will drop in to eat the peanut butter but then can't climb out because of the slick plastic walls.

Longer-Lasting Leather Work Gloves
Extend the life of leather work gloves with a light coating of silicone rubber sealer where the fingers and palm typically wear out first. Works especially well with split-leather gloves.

Easy Patch for Leaky Waders
To patch waders, first use sandpaper to rough up the rubber around the hole, clean with rubbing alcohol, let dry, and then apply 100-percent silicone rubber caulking. The patches hold surprisingly well, and the caulk costs less than $5 for a 10-ounce tube, more than enough to patch dozens of leaks.

Slick Boots Easier to Pull On and Off

Spray the inside of waders or rubber overshoes with Armor-All or a similar automotive rubber treatment, and they will be much easier to pull on and take off over shoes.

Make a Magnum Carry Bucket from a 55-Gallon Drum

To make a BIG bucket, cut down a 55-gallon plastic barrel in the desired size, leaving handles on opposing sides. If you want water to drain out, drill holes in the bottom.

Mouse-Proof Outhouse Toilet Paper

To prevent rodents trashing the toilet paper in an outhouse, keep the roll in a 26-ounce coffee can with a lid. Fits perfectly.

Paint a Pair of Brush-Busting Britches

To make a pair of brush-busting britches out of an old pair of jeans, paint the fronts with oil-base enamel floor paint. (Don't paint the backs or the pants won't flex enough to be comfortable.) Two or three coats should do it.

Stove Screw Ice Cleats

Instead of hassling with ice cleats, use a nut driver to put 1/4-inch stove screws in a pair of old but still thick-soled boots. Check the wear pattern to locate the best places for the screws in the sole; a half-dozen should do the trick.

Save Felt Boot Liners with Duct Tape

Before putting a felt liner in a boot, place a couple of strips of duct tape across the back and lengthwise down the back. This keeps the felt from falling apart and also makes it easier to slip the boots on and off without the liners binding.

Leaky Gauntlets Still Good for Picking Berries

Old shoulder-length gauntlet gloves that leak are still good for picking blackberries. With one gauntlet on, part the sticker bushes then reach in with your other hand and pick the berries.

Garbage Bag Cover-All Keeps Clothes Clean

A cut in the center of the bottom for your head and one at each corner for an arm turns a large garbage bag into a pullover garment that will keep your clothing clean while fleshing hides, cleaning fish, etc.

Latex Liners for Leaky Gauntlets

Rather than discard a pair of shoulder-length trapping gauntlets that have a few small leaks, wear a pair of disposable latex gloves inside them. May not hold up to heavy trapline use, but my hands stay warm and dry while washing the truck.

Sheet Metal Handle Guard for Axe or Maul

To prevent the handle of an axe or maul breaking when you overreach and smack it on a block of wood, wrap the handle next to the head with heavy galvanized sheet metal and then bolt the metal securely in place.

Low-Cost Parachute Cord Boot Laces

Make custom bootlaces from parachute cord. It is available at most hardware stores for about 5 cents a foot. Simply cut to the desired length and then melt the tips to stop fraying. Outlasts store-bought laces, and looks just as good.

WD-40 Keeps Car Doors from Freezing Shut

To prevent being frozen out of your vehicle, spray the door locks and hinges with WD-40. Also spray some on a rag and wipe the rubber doorjambs.

Super Glue Helps Cracked Hands Heal

During winter my hands get so dry from outdoor work they crack and won't heal. A drop of super glue on each crack (on clean, dry hands) protects and lets it heal while reducing the pain. The glue lasts longer, is cheaper and more effective than Band-Aids.

Carabiner Spare Key Keeper

Use a small carabiner key ring to clip a spare key in the front wheel well where it is hidden yet accessible.

Patch Rubber Waders with Goop and Inner Tube
To patch rubber waders, apply Goop shoe repair under a piece of bicycle inner tube. Add an "overpatch" at stress areas, such as the knee, and you may prevent leaks before they happen. The patches stay flexible and last forever.

Recycle Felt Boot Liners as Insoles
When the felt liners in Sorrel boots wear out on the bottoms, remove them, mark and cut out foot-shaped insoles from the good material in the upper part. Place these "insoles" back in the bottoms of the boots (one or two thick) before putting in new felts. Gives extra cushion and insulation where you need it, and extends the life of the new liners.

Styling Outdoors in Second-Hand Wool Suit Pants
Wool pants are great for cold, damp weather, but they can be expensive. I pick up just the pants from wool dress suits at the local secondhand shop and pay $4 a pair. At that price, I can afford to be the best-dressed guy afield.

Trailer Light Outlet Works for Power Winch, Too
You may not have to run a second set of wires to mount a power winch to the back of a truck. Just use the trailer light outlet. Simply buy a plug and wire the winch to the ground and auxiliary slots of the plug.

Ice Jugs in the Freezer Save Money
Buy your next chest freezer bigger than what you need and line the bottom with old plastic milk jugs about three quarters of the way filled with water. The freezer will use less electricity, and should the power go out, you have a big icebox that will keep things fresh for a very long time.

Add a Little Kerosene to Winter Chain Saw Oil
In extreme cold, chain saw bar oil can thicken to the point it is

difficult to pour. For such cold days, keep a separate quart of oil thinned with a small amount of kerosene.

Minnow Trap Doubles for Mice
Put a little dog food in a minnow trap (the cylinder kind with funnels on each end) and it may also serve as a mousetrap in a barn or outbuilding.

Recycle Meat Trays into Boot Insoles
The plastic foam trays meat comes packaged on at the grocery store can be quickly cut into boot insoles. Simply trace the outline of your foot and then trim to fit the boot. Makes old boots warm and comfortable again.

Vise Grips Make a Great Nut Buster
Black walnuts and butternuts can be easily cracked with a pair of vise grips. With the right adjustments they come out in quarters, and cleanup is easy if you hold the nuts over a cardboard box while cracking.

Sumac Makes Natural Maple Taps
Six-inch sections of sumac branch may be used to tap maple trees. The pithy centers are easily removed with a 1/4-inch drill bit. Sharpen one end to a blunt point, and drill a hole in the maple tree just tight enough to insert the sumac spigot. There should be little if any leakage, and the sumac spigots may be stored indoors and reused year after year.

Swiss Army Knife Knot-Picker
The toughest knot, even soaked cotton shoelaces, can be picked loose with the small corkscrew on a Swiss army pocketknife. Use the point to pry open strands, and then twist the point through the knot and tug.

Brass Brush Good for Cleaning More than Guns
I carry a .22 rifle cleaning brush in my toolbox. It comes in handy for cleaning out corrosion in trailer light plugs, etc. Just

insert and twist.

Ice Jugs Keep Dog Water Cool
To keep a dog's water cool and refreshing on a hot day, fill 1-gallon milk jugs with water, freeze them, and drop one like a big ice cube in the 5-gallon water bucket.

Peanut Oil Preserves Leather Knife Handles, Sheaths
To prevent the leather washers on a knife handle drying and cracking, soak the knife overnight in peanut oil. Also do this with leather sheaths. It saturates the leather, making it water- and rot-resistant. One soaking should be good for many years.

Super-Braid Fishing Line Makes Super Thread, Too
The Kevlar super-braid fishing lines make super thread for sewing leather, canvas and other heavy-duty fabrics. Just save the pieces you cut off when untangling knots, etc.

Dipstick a Handy Source for "Breaking" Oil
To free up a seized item in the field, such as the pump on a gas lantern, pull the dipstick from your car motor and let a few drops of oil drip on the problem. Warm engine oil frees 'most anything.

Ratchet Strap Doubles as Come-Along
A ratcheting tie-down strap makes a great little come-along for an ATV or a snowmobile. It has surprising pulling power, is lightweight and compact in a toolbox.

Sew with Fishing Line and a Hook
If you need to repair something with a rough sewing job, and don't have a needle and thread, use fishing line and a hook for a needle, either as is or straightened out.

BB Clean Hummingbird Feeder
To clean a hummingbird feeder (or 'most any glass bottle) fill with warm water and a little dishwashing soap then drop in a couple of ounces of BB shot. Swirl the shot in a circular motion

until the glass comes clean, dump out and rinse.

Nail Aprons Add Pockets to Pails
To add four roomy pockets to a 5-gallon tote pail, tie a couple of carpenter's nail aprons on opposite sides. The aprons are free or offered for a nominal cost at most lumberyards.

Apply Antiperspirant on Your Feet
Before putting on cold weather footwear, apply underarm antiperspirant to your feet. Reducing perspiration will keep your feet drier and warmer.

Recycle Inner Tube as Bungee Cords
To make a custom bungee cord from an old bicycle inner tube, just cut the tube to the desired length, punch holes through both ends and insert S-hooks (available for little cost at any hardware store). Also can be used as a bumper between a tent or tarp rope and a ground peg, reducing wear on the grommet.

Ironing Board Makes a Stand-Up Table
Remove the pad and cover from an old ironing board, glue or screw a cutting board on top, and you have an adjustable-height table that is ideal for cleaning fish and game while standing up; it washes up easily with soap and water then folds flat for storage. A large, flat spring clamp can be bolted on for holding fish or game in place. With the addition of sandbags, you have a portable, adjustable shooting bench, too.

Pop Bottles Keep Boots and Waders in Shape
To help waders and knee-high boots keep their shape during storage, slip a couple of empty 2-liter pop bottles into them. Reduces leaks at the ankles where boots tend to fold over and crack, and also makes the boots easier to slip onto your feet.

Bar Soap Plugs Small Gas and Oil Leaks
Keep a bar of soap in your vehicle or boat and you can use it to plug small holes in oil pans and gas tanks. Just rub the soap into

the hole or crack until it stops leaking.

Recycle Old Waders as Waterproof Knee Patches
Cut the good material out of old hip boots or waders and use it to make waterproof patches to sew on the knees of work pants, ice-fishing suits, trapping coveralls, etc. Keeps knees dry while kneeling on ice, snow or wet ground.

Paintbrush Handle Makes Ax File Safer
An old paintbrush handle makes a great addition to an ax-sharpening file, protecting fingers and hands.

Seal Boots with Duct Tape
Wrap duct tape around bottom of pants leg, boot top and laces before going afield. Debris won't slide down inside the boot, ticks won't climb up inside the pants leg, and the laces will remain tied through the snaggiest briar patch.

Wood Stove Preserver
Add several inches of sand to the bottom of the firebox of a wood stove, outdoor grill or smoker, and the metal underside will last much longer.

Use Baking Soda to Dry-Clean a Dog
You can "dry clean" a smelly old dog by working baking soda into its fur and then brushing it out.

Escape Mud Holes with Concrete Reinforcing Mesh
Carry a couple of pieces of concrete reinforcing steel mesh in your pickup truck. If you get stuck in mud, simply wedge it under the drive wheels and you may be able to pull right out.

Carpet Scraps Keep Toes Warm & Dry
Cut carpet scraps to the size of your outlined foot and stick in waders or hip boots. Keeps toes warm and dry, and if you make several pairs, you can change them as they get damp.

Frozen Firewood Easier to Split

Logs split easiest when frozen, with the butt end up. The wedge or axe then splits with the grain of the limbs, not against.

Boots Slide on Easier Over Grocery Bags

Place a thin plastic grocery bag over your socked foot, and a rubber boot will slide on much easier.

Old Cell Phones Still Always on Call

By law, all cell phones must be able to access emergency numbers, whether or not you pay for service. Keep an old cell phone and charger in your truck. If you get into trouble, help is at your fingertips.

Feed Bags Great for Bulk Storage

Woven plastic grain feed sacks are great for storing clothing, boots and other outdoor gear. Just shake out the dust and run through the washer. They also work well as meat bags for hauling big-game quarters out of the woods.

Fruit Carton Fire Starters

The cartons in which fruit is shipped, the thick ones with wax coating, make great fire starting material. Cut 3-inch squares and then make several cuts in but not completely through each square. Now bend up the cuts like the petals of a flower. Will light in damp or windy conditions, and the wax keeps it going until kindling ignites. Grocery stores gladly give them away.

Baby Wipes Also Good for Cleaning Hands

Toss a compact pop-up container of baby wipes in your kit and use them to clean your hands anywhere.

Ways to Recycle Flexible Tent Poles

Free-standing dome tents wear out. But the flexible fiberglass poles last forever, and if you bend one in a half-circle above a cabin's corner wood stove, it makes a great rack to dry wet gear. After you bend it in a half-circle, drill a couple of holes in the wall where the pole touches, insert the ends of the pole into these holes and use wire or small chain to attach to the ceiling out at the middle of the bow. The poles break down for easy carry, and because they have an elastic shock cord, they reassemble instantly. With camo cloth, you can assemble a custom ground blind in a minute or less.

Super Easy Siphon Starter

For easier siphoning of fuel or any other liquid, attach a piece of cloth to the end of a wire and thread the wire through the siphon hose. Insert the end of the hose with the cloth stopper into the liquid and use the wire to pull the cloth stopper up and through the hose. If the wet cloth fits tightly enough, the vacuum will pull the liquid up the hose and start the siphon.

Edible Olive Oil for Knives, etc.

After cleaning, coat knives, meat grinder plates, etc., with olive oil. Prevents rust, is completely edible, and won't gum up like vegetable or corn oil.

Use Dish Soap for Fog-Free Windows

To prevent windows fogging on cold, damp days, squeeze a little dish soap on a dry rag and wipe down the glass. May have to be repeated from time to time, but it works.

Use Boot Laces to Hold Up Socks

To prevent socks slipping down in boots and balling up underfoot, work one end of the boot lace through the fabric of the sock before tying the boot. The sock won't slip.

Sewn-In Pocket Sheath

To better carry a big pocketknife in a front pants pocket, sew a sheath right into the pocket. Keeps the knife upright and out of the way, leaving more room for other things.

Axe Handle Soak a Swell Idea

Soaking axe handles in water to make them swell and fit tighter to the head is a good idea, but if you use antifreeze instead of water, the glycerin in the antifreeze will not dry out, and it's a permanent one-time application.

Stuff Leather Boots with Newspaper
When packing away leather boots, stuff them with newspaper. Helps the boot retain its shape without creasing, which prolongs the life of the leather.

Cinnamon a Spicy Ant Repellent
Sprinkle enough cinnamon around a building, and ants will stay out. Put it directly on an anthill, and they'll move out. It's safe should children or pets be exposed, and bought in bulk, cheaper than a commercial pesticide.

Squirt Bottle for Chain Saw Oil
Put chain saw bar oil in a clean plastic syrup bottle with a snap cap. It won't leak if it falls over and neatly fills the oil reservoir on the saw with little if any overflow. Easy to refill, and you can tell at a glance how much oil is in the bottle.

Duct Tape Keeps Snow Out of Boots
Before walking in deep snow, wrap duct tape where your pants legs meet the boot tops to keep out the snow.

.22 Quick Fix for Loose Axe Head
To quickly tighten a loose axe head, shoot up some .22 ammo and wedge the spent cartridges in between the wood handle and the metal head (drive them in primer side up).

Flipping Extends Life of Chain Saw Bar
To make a new chain saw bar last four to six times longer, every time you touch up or sharpen the chain, turn the bar over; it only takes an extra minute or so. The reason this works is you cut with the bottom side probably 95 percent of the time or more. By flipping the bar, you even the wear.

Easy Light for Pickup Cap

Battery-powered closet lights also work great to light pickup caps. Find one that hooks onto a closet rod and you can just hang it on a brace of the truck cap.

Recycle Old Socks into Gaiters

Cut the toes off old socks to make snow gaiters. Works especially well over cross-country ski shoes.

Crossing Barbed Wire with Bungee Cords

Two short, strong bungee cords make it easier to pass through a barbed wire fence. Hook both cords on the middle wire, pull down and hook the other ends of the cords on the bottom wire. Opens space between the top and middle wire that you then may step and duck through.

Weigh Ginseng at Grocery Store Meat Counter

Before shipping wild ginseng, I take it to the local market and have it weighed on the meat counter's digital scales. The scale prints a stick-on tag that lists the weight to within a tenth of an ounce. Placed as a seal on the closed bag, this tells the buyer I knew the precise weight when I shipped. At $300 a pound, fractions of ounces add up fast.

10-Year Rubber Wader Care

To get 10 years out of a pair of rubber waders, at the start of each season wipe with an auto vinyl protector, such as Armor-All. At the end of the season, thoroughly clean and apply protector again. Then pack the insides with newspaper (to avoid creasing) and hang in a large black trash bag (to avoid ultraviolet light).

Make a Taller Bucket

Cut just the bottom off a 5-gallon plastic bucket, caulk all the way around the outside of the cut bucket's bottom edge with liquid cement, and slide this inside another whole bucket. Slide up or down to adjust to the desired depth/height, let dry overnight, and you have a taller version of the regular 5-gallon bucket. Perfect for packing two-piece fishing poles, trap stakes, etc.

Coffee Cup Knife Sharpener
There is a handy knife sharpener on the bottom of every ceramic coffee cup. The cups are made of the same material as ceramic sharpening stones and some sharpening steels, and the ring around the bottom is not glazed, leaving abrasive material exposed. Just turn the cup over and you have a ring-shaped, medium-grit sharpening stone.

Reversible Wear Pocket Warmers
When wearing reversible outerwear in winter, put disposable hand warmers in the inside pockets. They can't fall out, and the outer pockets will be empty and plenty warm for your hands.

Warm & Comfy Dog Bed
To make a durable, comfortable bed for an outside dog house, fill a gunny sack half full of Styrofoam packing peanuts and sew the top closed. Save the cut-off ends of long flea collars and toss those in, too, before sewing. Water drains through the peanuts, and the dog's body heat dries the cover. Styrofoam also insulates, keeping the dog warmer in the winter. To wash, simply shampoo, hose down, and hang to dry.

Use Gutter Spikes for Safety Ice Spikes
Before walking on a frozen lake, duct tape a 7-inch knurled hardened-aluminum rain gutter spike (point down) to each arm of your coat. You'll soon forget they're there, but if you ever fall through the ice, they can be pulled off instantly and used as ice picks to help pull yourself back up on the ice.

ATV Locked & Loaded
To secure a four-wheel ATV in the bed of a pickup truck, attach a trailer ball receiver to a large hinge and then mount the hinge in the pickup box (a backing plate may be required) directly below the cab's rear window at the same height as the ATV's trailer-pulling hitch ball (most ATVs come with a ball on the back for

towing small trailers). When not in use, the hinged receiver hangs down out of the way. When the ATV is backed onto the pickup bed, the receiver is raised and locked on the hitch ball.

Chlorine Bleach Soak Relieves Insect Bite Itch

To relieve the itch from chiggers and other biting insects, pour 3 capfuls of chlorine bleach into a bathtub of warm water. Soak for 15 to 25 minutes. If you scratch the bites first, the bleach will sting but do a better job.

Bait Mousetraps with Kibble

To catch a mouse that steals other baits, use fine wire to attach a piece of kibble-style dry dog food to a mousetrap trigger. The biscuit-shaped kibbles are easiest to tie, but you can put a groove in a round one. It takes an extra minute, but you don't have to rebait as often, and one kibble may catch half a dozen mice.

Check for Wader Leaks with a Trouble Light

To find tiny leaks and worn places in waders, take them in a dark room and put a trouble light inside them. The light will shine through to reveal any bad spots.

Patch Waders with Duct Tape

Duct tape is the quickest and easiest way to patch a small leak in rubber waders. Thoroughly dry the area around the hole before applying the tape, and it will hold for a long time.

Clear Packing Tape Screen Saver

Place clear packaging tape over the soft plastic viewing screens of electronic devices you carry in the field (GPS, digital camera, etc.). It costs next to nothing, and if you hold the tape on tight and move your fingers back and forth, you can apply it without air bubbles. It is nearly invisible and protects the screen from scratches. If the tape gets marred, just replace with a fresh piece.

Remove Leather Keychain Before Hiding Keys

If you like to hide car keys in the woods rather than risk dropping them, remove any leather keychain, first. Leather is tasty to small critters. We returned from a 2-day canoe trip to find our keys not where we left them but 100 feet away—with the leather key tag completely chewed away.

Burn the Creosote Out of a Stove Pipe

To clean the creosote out of a stove pipe, dismantle and stuff crumpled newspaper inside the sections. Light the paper on one end and let it burn through to the other end. Let the pipe cool, and the bubbled-up creosote will be easier to scrape out. Repeat as many times as is necessary to remove the creosote. But always do it outside, and be careful. The pipe gets very hot.

Rolled Up Newspaper Knife Strop

After you sharpen a knife on the finest stone, get a razor-fine edge by stropping the blade on a rolled up newspaper with blade edge towards you, pushing the knife away, first one side and then the other.

Monofilament Line Prevents Loose Screws

To make a bolt, nut or screw hold better, wrap a small piece of monofilament fishing line in the threads before tightening it down. Works great and can be removed easily.

Spark Plug Gapper Makes a Keychain Screwdriver

The round spark plug gap tools sold for $1 or less at auto parts stores make handy key chain screwdrivers. Perforated for chain carry, they range from .020 to .100 around the rim, so they fit a variety of screw slot sizes. Only 1-1/2 inches in diameter yet capable of producing considerable leverage and torque.

Flat-Proof Wheelbarrow Tires

To prevent wheelbarrow tires going flat, fill with the expanding foam insulation sold to seal gaps around windows, etc. Remove the valve stem guts, slide the applicator hose over the valve stem, and inject the foam straight into the tire (one can per tire). Have the valve guts ready to re-install quickly, and expect some foam to squirt out under pressure. A rag with mineral spirits cleans off the foam. Spin the tire as it hardens to avoid flat spots.

Plywood Truck Bed Organizer
Cut a sheet of 3/4-inch plywood to match the bed of your pickup truck. Then, in the plywood cut round holes a little bigger than 5-gallon buckets and square holes a little bigger than plastic milk crates. Keeps the buckets and crates from sliding around and tipping over. Position the holes around the outside of the bed, and the buckets and crates will be within easy reach. "Custom" holes can be cut to hold coolers and other items.

Bar Stool Cushion Makes a Cushy Bucket Seat
To put a comfortable seat on a 5-gallon bucket, use an elastic-bottom bar stool cushion. Fits a 5-gallon bucket lid, and they come in a variety of thicknesses and colors.

Snow-Free with WD-40
To prevent snow sticking to snowshoes, skis, shovels, etc., spray WD-40 on the problem areas before use.

Cream Hand Cleaner Restores Whetstone
When a whetstone becomes clogged with steel filings and oily grime, switch to cream hand cleaner instead of oil for sharpening knives, and that will clean out the pores until the whetstone again cuts like new.

Campho-Phenique Keeps Out Insects & Rodents
Before storing gear in a box or other compartment, open a bottle of Campho-Phenique and put it inside to keep mice and insects outside. Tape the bottle upright so it won't tip and spill.

Vacuum Packer Speeds Up Jerky Marinade
Speed up the marinating of jerky meat by vacuum packing it with the marinade. The meat will then suck up the marinade, and you can start to dehydrate it in 2 hours instead of 2 days. It's ready to go as soon as the meat is no longer blood red.

Use Duct Tape to Remove Shed Hair

Duct tape works great for removing shed pet hair from clothing and upholstery. Just press lightly and then pull up.

Recycle Leather Belt into a Dog Collar

Instead of throwing away worn-out leather belts, cut off the bad end to your dog's neck size and then punch new holes in the leather for the buckle.

Lifelong Lawn Mower Cord Boot Laces

For extra-durable bootlaces, use a lawn mower pull cord. Sold inexpensively in different diameters at lawn mower repair shops, and all should outlast the boot itself.

Stretching a Shoestring Budget

When you first see a boot lace fraying around a boot eye, loosen the lace and move the frayed part into the center between two eyes. Lasts about as long as putting in a new lace.

Use Newspaper to Dry Dog

Instead of getting towels stinky drying off dogs, use old newspaper wadded into balls. Dries the dog quickly, and then you throw away the mess. (Works for trapped fur, too.)

Tomato Restores Brass Shine

To clean brass, soak it in tomato juice overnight. Rinse in hot water, and it shines like new.

Mark the Blade to Hold the Edge

Knife blades are sharpened at different angles. When time comes to touch up a blade, color both sides of the entire length of the cutting edge with a dark marker. While honing, watch where the color is removed to maintain the proper angle.

Roof Shingles Free Stuck Vehicle

Carry some roofing shingles in your car trunk or truck bed. When you get stuck in slick mud, ice or snow, wedge a shingle in front of the drive wheel, rough side down, and the tire will get instant traction.

Sack Those Wild 'Shrooms
When picking wild mushrooms, put them in onion sacks or orange sacks made from nylon netting. This lets the spores drop back on the woods floor, not down the drain at home.

Pack a Shower Cap for Unexpected Rain
Throw-away clear plastic shower caps cost almost nothing, take up little room in a pocket or pack, and will keep your head dry during an unexpected rain. Can be worn under a cloth cap or fitted overtop.

Snaky Rope Spooks Geese Off Walkways
To keep wild geese from leaving a mess of droppings on your sidewalks and driveway, tie knots in the ends of lengths of 1-inch rope and lay them on the driveway in snake-like curves. Geese will not cross over these ropes, perhaps thinking they are snakes.

Shoe GOO Super Patching Compound
For a quick and permanent patch of everything from tents to blue jeans, apply a thin layer of Shoe GOO adhesive on the underside of the torn material and then press on a piece of patch material. Center the patch and press firmly.

Mesh Decoy Bag Doubles for Wild Roots
A mesh decoy bag with back straps makes a great collecting sack when digging roots. While you walk around the woods with your harvest, the dirt falls out.

Tape Holds Ticks Picked off Dogs
Before sitting down to pick the ticks off of a dog, grab a dispenser of transparent tape. As you remove each tick, stick it on the sticky side of the tape and then fold the tape over the tick. No lost ticks, and easy to discard.

A Boot Lace Tie that Binds

For a boot lace knot that holds like a double knot yet is easy to untie, start the same as when making a regular single knot, but after forming the first loop, pass the shoestring around that loop twice instead of once before forming and pulling the second loop through. To undo, just pull on a shoestring end same as when undoing a single knot. Even a wet knot unties quickly and easily.

Repel Biting Bugs Without Spraying Your Face

To stop deer flies and black gnats biting your face, spray the edges of a bandanna handkerchief with repellent and put it over your head with one point in front. Now put on a cap to hold it in place. Works reasonably well, and you don't have to spray the chemicals directly on your face.

Lemon Juice Breaks a Barking Dog

If you want to break a dog from unwanted barking, squirt lemon juice into its mouth when it barks, with a stern command like "No!" They don't like the taste and soon figure out that if they don't bark, they won't get a mouthful.

Shoo Fly, Don't Circle Me

When swatting won't shoo away a pesky horsefly, lean back against the trunk of a tree. When the fly can no longer circle its prey (you), it gives up and flies away. Works every time.

Cornmeal Ant Killer

To get rid of ants, sprinkle cornmeal where you see them; ants eat it but can't digest it. Might take a couple of weeks, but it is safer and cheaper than poison, and it works.

Recap Bootlaces with Heat Shrink Tubing

When bootlaces fray on the ends, use heat-shrink tubing to re-cap them. Inexpensive packages with assorted sizes are sold at electronics supply stores. Cut off the frayed end of the lace, slip on the tightest tube that still fits, trim to length and then heat with a lighter.

Inner Tube Sections Improve Grip on Flashlight
To improve your grip on a metal tube-style D-cell flashlight, cut an old bicycle inner tube into cross-section rings 3 or 4 inches wide and slide these onto the flashlight. Voila! No more slipping.

Recycle Old Waders into Chaps
Leaky, worn-out waders make terrific chaps; they fend off thorns, help keep pants dry, and also deflect ticks and chiggers. Just lop off the boot parts and wear the legs over your regular pants and boots.

Rubber Roof Truck Bed Liner
Cut a piece of rubber roofing material to fit the bed of your pickup truck; it stops objects sliding around and also protects somewhat like a bed liner.

Slip Hip Waders on Over Garbage Bags
If you have trouble sliding hip waders on and off, put each foot and leg in 30-gallon plastic trash bags before pulling on the waders. They fit in hip waders like a glove and allow you to slip the waders on and off with ease.

Flour Stops Bleeding of Short-Clipped Dog Nail
If you cut a dog's toenail too short it will bleed. Dip it in flour to help stop that bleeding.

Baby Oil Burr Remover
Plain old baby oil works better than anything on the market to remove cockle burrs from the tails of dogs, horses and even the pelts of furbearers like coyotes.

Rubber Band Pocketknife Retainer
To prevent a pocketknife slipping out of a pants pocket, double-wrap a rubber band around it.

Vinegar & Mineral Oil Porcupine Quill Removal
Vinegar and mineral oil make it easier to pull porcupine quills

from a dog. Pour vinegar where the quill enters the skin. Wait 5 to 10 minutes and repeat. A few minutes after the second application, pour mineral oil over the quill. The vinegar softens the quill, and the oil helps it pop out more easily with less pain.

Preparation H Good for Insect Bites, Too
Preparation H works great on insect bites (especially black fly bites). Just like the commercials say, it stops the itch and reduces the swelling.

Hot Pepper & Peanut Butter Balls Repel Squirrels
Mix very hot pepper in balls of peanut butter and drop around the plants to keep the squirrels out of your tomatoes.

Make Disposable Apron from a Garbage Bag
A 33-gallon plastic trash bag with drawstrings makes an instant disposable apron for cleaning fish, game, or skinning furbearers. Pull the drawstrings out like it was full of trash and put them over your head and around your neck. Secure at the middle with a bungee cord wrapped around your waist and let the rest hang down to your knees. When you're finished, turn the bag inside out and fill it with the remains.

Put Propane Tank in Milk Crate to Prevent Rolling
To prevent a propane tank rolling around in the back of a truck, place it in a plastic milk crate.

Air-Tight Storage Best for Rubber Waders, Etc.
Exposure to the ozone in the air accelerates the deterioration of waders and other rubber gear. To reduce this, store between seasons in sealed plastic bags.

Super Glue ATV Tire Patch
Carry a big tube of super glue and an air pump on your ATV. Should you get a flat tire, find the leak, shoot glue in the hole, and then use a twig to really work it in. Repeat twice, allowing the glue to set up each time. Finish by smearing glue all over the

outside of the sealed hole. Holds about as well as a patch kit.

Fly-Catcher Strip Good for Wasps & Hornets, Too
To get rid of a hornet or wasp nest where you don't want to spray strong poison, thumbtack a fly-catching ribbon to the end of a long bamboo pole (or other long pole) and wrap the rest of the ribbon down around the pole. Hold the end of the ribbon in place with a rubber band. Put it up by the nest, and all of the hornets or wasps will be caught in a short time.

Refrigerator Fan Gently Dries Leather Boots
Place a wet leather boot on its side on the floor, open end facing a refrigerator. The gentle flow of warm air from the compressor will dry the boot without damaging the leather or other materials.

Milk Jug Makes a Great Berry Picking Bucket
For a handy berry-picking bucket, cut a hand-size opening in the top of a 1-gallon plastic milk jug, leaving the handle attached. You can run a belt through the handle for hands-free carry and two-handed picking.

Buttermilk Washes Out Walnut Stains
When picking up walnuts, the dye in the hulls will stain your fingers, and it will not wash off with soap and water. But it will wash off with buttermilk.

Silicone Slicks Up Ratchet Tie-Downs
Spray ratchet tie-downs with silicone lubricant and you won't believe how much smoother they work.

Chapstick® as Emergency Lubricant
Chapstick works like a charm as a lubricant for zippers and such when other products aren't handy.

Pack an Emergency Umbrella
Put a small, compact folding umbrella in your pack. Weighs almost nothing, deploys instantly, and will keep you dry.

Weed Whacker Line Ideal for Feeding Drawstrings
When replacing the drawstring in a hooded sweatshirt, tent bag, etc., first feed the stiff line from a weed whacker through the opening and out the other end. Tape the new drawstring to the end of this line and pull it back through.

Recycle Push-Spigot Soap Bottle as Water Bottle
After using the detergent in a plastic bottle with a push-button spigot, rinse it out thoroughly, fill with water, and toss in the back of the truck. Comes in handy to wash hands after skinning furbearers, cleaning fish or game. Also comes in handy for giving the dog a quick drink. The bottles are sturdy, and the spigots rarely leak.

Untie Cinched Knots with Needle-Nose Vise Grips
Needle-nose vise grip pliers are perfect for untying cinched down rope knots.

Dryer Sheet Keeps Gear Soft and Mouse-Free
To keep mice out of gear stored during the off-season, pack it away with a sheet of the fabric softener that goes in clothes dryers. They can't stand that smell.

Recycle Old Toothbrushes
Old toothbrushes are great for working paste waterproofing into the seam between the sole and leather of a hunting boot. Great for cleaning small, hard-to-reach gun parts, too. Before repacking wheel bearings, dip a toothbrush in gasoline and scrub the old grease out of the bearings and races; really gets into the nooks and crannies.

Trash Bag Waders
If you know you will have to cross a wet ditch or small stream in the middle of a longer hike, instead of packing heavy waders, put a pair of old tennis shoes and two 13-gallon trash bags in your pack. At the crossing, take off your hiking boots, slip stockinged feet in the trash bags, tie them up around your legs with the

drawstrings, put on the tennis shoes, and wade across.

Nylon Pants a Slick Tick Solution
When hiking in tick country, don't wear jeans or anything else made of cotton. Ticks can grab this material and climb with ease. Instead, wear slick nylon pants with elastic bands at the cuffs.

Knee-High Nylons Make Boots Easy On, Easy Off
Wear knee-high women's nylon hose over your heavy, insulated socks. Adds a layer of warmth, and boots slide on and off so easily you won't need a bootjack.

Rebar Stakes for Winching ATV Out of Muck
A 36-inch stake of 3/4-inch rebar can serve as an anchor for winching out an ATV where there is nowhere else to attach the cable. Just drive the stake in the ground at an angle away from the ATV and slip on the cable end loop over the top.

Buy Garage Sale Leather for Sheaths
Used but like-new leather purses go for almost nothing at garage and rummage sales, often a dollar or less. Yet some are made of very high-quality leather that can be used to make excellent axe and knife sheaths.

Panty Hose Keep Even Macho Men Warm
If you aren't too macho to give it a try, try women's panty hose under your long johns. You won't believe how much warmer you'll be, and they're cheap, too.

Paint Roller Pan a Good Parts Catcher
When taking apart a fishing reel or other intricate mechanism, do it over a clean paint roller pan to catch any small screws or other parts that may fall out.

Lexel® Sealant for Waders and Everything Else
Lexel Sealant, the all-purpose product sold at home building supply stores, is the best waterproof repair product for waders,

boots, tents, period. It's clear and very flexible, will not peel or crack, and can even be applied straight on a wet surface. A pair of old trapping hip boots repaired on the 'line two years ago still don't leak.

Apply Iodine First for Easier Splinter Removal

When you have a splinter to remove, first dab it with iodine to sterilize the spot and also stain the splinter, making it easier to see and remove.

Chemical Hand Warmers Can Be Saved for Later

If a disposable chemical hand warmer is still heating when you are done for the day, place it in a sealable plastic bag, squeeze out the air, and seal. Stops the heat-generating chemical reaction, and the warmer can be reused because it will heat back up when again exposed to air.

Soft Plastic Patch for Neoprene Waders

To repair a small leak in neoprene waders, hold an open flame to the tip of a soft plastic fishing bait and let the melting plastic drip onto the leak. Once it dries, the waders are again waterproof.

Lint Roller Picks Off Ticks and Mites

A lint roller is great for removing tiny deer ticks and turkey mites from skin and clothing. A new sheet tears off about every 6 inches, and you may be amazed (or disgusted) by what you see.

Birdhouse Rodent-Only Poison Dispenser

To keep cats and dogs out of mouse poison, put it in a birdhouse with a small entry opening. Mice and even rats may use the small hole, but not cats or dogs.

Cooking Spray Doubles as Waterproof Lubricant

Non-stick cooking spray works about as well as expensive waterproofing products for boots, snowshoe bindings, etc., and is a lot less expensive. Also works as a lubricant for sleeping bag and tent zippers.

Dust Off Chiggers & Ticks
To repel chiggers and ticks, dust your clothes and skin with flowers of sulfur (sulfur sublimed) from the local pharmacy. Apply especially well at the openings of pant legs, shirtsleeves and at the neck. You may still see ticks on your clothes but not attached to your skin. It has little odor and washes off easily.

Rice Dries Wet Electronics
Should a cell phone or GPS get wet, turn it off immediately, and as soon as possible, put it in a bag of uncooked white rice for at least 24 hours; the rice draws out the moisture, preventing further damage.

Taxidermy Duster in a Can
Compressed air in a spray can (sold for cleaning electronics) will also clean taxidermy mounts. Approach slowly to find the right distance from can to mount and then blow the feathers, fur or scales to safely clean and groom.

Dollar Bill Doubles as 6-inch Ruler
If you don't have a tape measure handy, you can "guesstimate" lengths with fair accuracy using a dollar bill, which is just slightly over 6 inches long.

Freeze-Proof Your Rain Gauge
To prevent a rain gauge freezing, fill it to an even number with RV antifreeze and then subtract that from the total when reading the gauge.

Freezer Good for Freeze-Proof Storage, Too
An old upright freezer works great for storing canned goods, homegrown potatoes, etc., over winter in an unheated space. Turn the temperature all the way up, and nothing freezes. The light still comes on when the door opens.

Corncob Fire Starters
To make low-cost fire starters, soak dry corncobs in kerosene for

5 minutes. (Do not use gasoline.) Lift the cobs from the kerosene and let any excess drain back into the kerosene container. After 5 minutes of draining, place the treated cobs in sealable gallon freezer bags; a dozen should fit easily. Store outside by the woodpile, and use two to start each fire.

Ammonia Repels Unwanted "Visit" by Dog
If you are tired of the neighbor's dog urinating on your mailbox post, pour household ammonia around the bottom. It's cheap, and it usually works.

Camp Chair Carry Sacks Worth Keeping
The nylon stuff-sacks that fold-up camping chairs come in usually outlast the chairs. Then they are good for many other items, with a shoulder strap for comfortable carry.

Bag Boots Before Pulling Pants Over
If you already have your pants and boots on and then decide you want to wear camo pants over top, slide a plastic bag over your booted foot and the camo pants will pull over easily.

Holders Good for More than Cartridges
The shell holders from inside boxes of rifle cartridges also make handy workshop holders for pencils, drill bits, etc.

Make a Hiking Staff from a Sunflower Staff
For an unusual hiking staff, dry a sunflower stalk, coat twice with liquid wax, and add a rubber chair leg tip (available at any hardware store). Not as strong as hardwood but super light and still plenty stout. Your friends will never guess what it is.

Insulate that Outhouse Seat
To make an outhouse a little more inviting on a frosty winter morning, make a seat insulator by cutting a right-sized hole in a sheet of 1-inch blue insulation board or Styrofoam insulation and gluing it over the existing seat hole. There is no initial frost, and your own bottom will soon warm it nicely.

Wedge Makes Cinched Knot Not a Problem

To prevent a rope knot cinching down so tight you can't loosen it, tie it with a thin wedge of wood in the knot. Holds until you want to untie; then just pull out the wedge and the knot comes undone with ease.

Recycle Restaurant-Grade Wrap Tubes as Map Tubes

The tubes that restaurant-grade plastic food wrap comes on make great map tubes. All but indestructible, waterproof, and will hold several rolled-up topo maps. Ask a local restaurant manager to save them for you.

Liquid Soap Keeps Zippers Zipping

A little liquid hand soap will prevent zippers rusting and sticking.

Super Glue Restores Frayed Bootlaces

To fix frazzled boot lace ends so they can be fed back through eyelets, simply trim and apply a drop of super glue.

Inner Tube Makes Zippo Slip- and Water-Resistant

Zippo lighters are not waterproof and slide out of a pocket too easily. To fix both problems, cut a 1-inch section from a skinny bicycle inner tube and stretch this over the lighter so it covers the seam between the top and bottom and also the hinge. To use the lighter, just roll the band down like a turtleneck sweater. In a pinch, the inner tube will burn 2-1/2 minutes, making an emergency fire starter.

Garden Hose for Crossing Barbed Wire

Before throwing away a leaky old garden hose, cut off a 30-inch section, split it with a lengthwise cut, roll up and stow in your pack. The next time you need to cross barbed wire, slip this over the top strand and you will not snag your pants.

Clean Rusty Knife Blade with an Onion

Clean the rust from an old hunting knife blade by inserting it in an onion. Leave for a day and then slide it around inside the onion for a while. You should pull out a rust-free blade.

Beaver Sticks Make Great Garden Stakes
Beaver-stripped sticks make great garden stakes for tomatoes, peppers, pole beans, etc. Already trimmed and shaved.

Pick Off Ticks with Tape
Use a small piece of masking tape to pick off ticks that are not yet attached. They stick to the tape, and you can simply fold it over and throw it away without ever touching the tick.

Crack Nuts with a Bench Vise
Use a bench vise to crack walnuts and get complete halves or quarters with no smashed fingers and no flying fragments.

Old-Timey Wood Stain from Vinegar & Steel Wool
Stain for refinishing old gunstocks, knife handles and pack baskets may be made by immersing steel wool or scrap steel in a jar of vinegar. Let it soak for a week, and it will produce iron acetate, which stains wood gray. For darker stain, brush strong black tea onto the wood. After either stain dries, finish with boiled linseed oil.

Hand Cleaner Also Cleans Hone Stone
Pumice hand cleaner will quickly remove the dirty oil and metal shavings from a hone stone. Use an old toothbrush to work it into the stone with circular motions, then rinse.

Rope Caulk Seals Pickup Cap
A couple of dollars' worth of rope-type window caulk does a great job sealing a pickup-truck cap. Unroll, push down along the top of the truck bed where the cap sits, set the cap on and tighten the clamps.

Wear Latex Under Winter Gloves for Warmth
In extreme cold, wear a pair of disposable latex gloves under your regular gloves. The airtight barrier insulates without the

bulk of thicker gloves or mittens.

Dry Boots on Muskrat Stretchers
A clean wire muskrat stretcher makes an excellent boot dryer. Just slide it up in the wet boot and prop the boot over a furnace floor register.

Flea Collar Keeps Ticks and Chiggers Off
To keep chiggers and ticks at bay, wrap a small dog-size flea/tick collar around each pants leg (but not directly on your skin). At the end of the day, put in a sealed bag and save for the next trip outdoors. One collar may last all summer.

Use Rid® to Treat Chigger Bites
The best way to treat chiggers is to rub Rid® (or the generic equivalent) on the bites as soon as possible. The itch will be gone within 24 hours.

Shop Vac Sucks Up Hornets Coming & Going
Duct tape a shop vacuum's hose to the end of a long pole and use the pole to position the sucking end by the entrance to an unwanted hornet's nest. Turn on the vacuum, and let it get 'em coming and going. Before turning it off, spray strong insecticide down the hose. Leave outdoors where any escapees won't be a problem. After 24 hours, dump out the dead hornets.

Recycle Boot Socks to Close Coat Cuffs
When the heel wears out of a pair of heavy-duty boot socks, cut off the still-good upper legs and wear them around your wrists to cover the gaps between coat cuffs and gloves.

Use Binoculars Like a Magnifying Glass
You can use binoculars like a magnifying glass by turning them around and looking through the wrong end. Adjust the distance until you get the right eye relief, then move closer to the object being viewed until you get the desired magnification. Works great for digging a splinter out of a finger and similar situations.

Middle Knot Keeps Bootlaces Even

Bootlaces can be kept even in length simply by tying a square knot in the center of the lace between the bottom two eyelets. The knot stops the lace from slipping through either eye and out of place as you tighten and loosen the lace.

Dual Use for Dryer Sheets

The fabric softener sheets that go in the dryer will also repel biting insects. Just rub on exposed skin and then pin to the back of your cap. Works great.

Water Trees Straight to the Roots

Small trees suffer stress during long, hot, dry spells. To alleviate this, open two or three of the big 39-ounce coffee cans at both ends and then sink them about 2 inches into the ground beside the tree. Fill the cans with water and keep refilling until you are satisfied that the tree roots are well soaked. This saves water as it goes to the roots instead of evaporating off the surface.

Recycle Rubber Gloves into Magnum Rubber Bands

Cut cross sections from the wrists of old rubber gloves to make extra-strong rubber bands as wide and strong as you want.

Leave Dry Box Open to Save the O-Ring Seal

A dry box may leak after being stored too long with the lid closed, which causes compression "memory" of the O-ring gasket seal in the lid. When not in use, leave the box lid open.

Add Alligator Clip for Hands-Free Flashlight

Make a hands-free flashlight by duct taping an alligator clip to the barrel. Then it can be clipped onto brush or something almost anywhere.

Hose Makes Dog Chain Safer

Before staking out your dog, first run the chain through a length of old garden hose to keep it from tangling and injuring the dog.

Hang Waders to Store Without Cracking

To store waders so they don't fold and crack, bend a heavy wire coat hanger, drill holes in the heavy rubber heels to accommodate the ends of the wires, and hang boots by the heels, upside down.

Pin Hatchet Head to Hold in Place

To ensure that the head stays on a hatchet, drill a hole through the head and the handle then drive a split pin through the hole and ground the end off flush. For a snug fit, the split pin must match the drill bit size. The pin can be removed later with a punch, if need be.

PVC Pipe Whelping Puppy Protection Rail

To prevent a mother dog lying on a pile of pups and smothering one against the wall, make a puppy-safe guard rail from 1-inch PVC pipe. For a 4-foot whelping box, you will need 4 elbows, 16 Ts and 4-1/2 inch stubs to keep the rail off the floor and out from the wall. No need to glue, as the pipe fits so tightly it is hard to pull apart.

Longer Handle Improves Bucket Balance

To make a 5-gallon bucket less "tippy" when loaded with stakes and other tall gear, remove the short handle, drill a pair of holes on each side where the original handle was attached, and replace it with two longer rope handles. A piece of rope 24 inches long works well for each handle.

Recycle Inner Tube as Waterproof Knees

Cut a section of truck tire inner tube about a foot long and then slide it up over your pants leg and around your knees. The curve of the tube helps it hold comfortably in place, and it keeps pants dry when you kneel on damp ground.

Two-Point Hook-Up Better for Skidding Logs

A big log will skid better behind a tow vehicle with a two-point chain hook-up rather than a single chain. Wrap the chain around the log and hook it up about a foot from the end. Now run the chain to the tow vehicle, hook to the vehicle, and run the tag end of chain back to the log and hook it to chain wrap, on the opposite side of the log.

PVC Boot & Glove Drying Rack
Make a boot and glove power dryer out of PVC pipe and a hair dryer. The 1-1/2-inch pipe best fits most hair dryers. No need to glue the pieces as they fit snugly. Set on low, and it should safely dry boots and gloves in an hour or two.

Padded Axe Handle
To prevent an axe handle breaking when you miss a log with the head but strike it with the handle, slip 3 inches of radiator hose up onto the handle by the head and wrap liberally with duct tape to hold it in place. Also reduces the shock to your hands.

Make Dog House from a Plastic Storage Tub
Cut a door out of the side of a plastic storage tub to make an instant doghouse. Bolt on the lid and then turn it upside down. Pull the bolts to remove the lid/floor for easy cleaning. Drill holes at the corners of the lid and "lip" so rain quickly drains.

.22 Shell Works Well as Leather Punch
To make neat holes in leather belts, slings, etc., lay the leather on a board, stand a spent .22 casing (open end down) on the leather where you want the hole, and rap lightly with a hammer.

Prevent Cut Rope Fraying
After cutting rope to length for tie-downs and other uses, wrap the ends with strong thread, dip in head cement, and, after drying, coat with epoxy. The same process on a smaller scale puts new tips on frayed bootlaces.

Pop Bottle Sugar Sap Collector
To tap a maple tree for syrup-making sap, cut a 5-inch length of aluminum tubing to insert into the hole drilled in the trees. Then cut a slit in a plastic 2-liter pop bottle, push this on over the tube,

and tie it to the tree. Keeps out dirt and bugs. To drain the sap, simply untie the bottle, remove from tree and unscrew the cap.

Tie a Knife-Saving Knot

To prevent losing a knife should it slip out of a belt sheath, tie a leather lace around the top of the handle, tie a knot in the end of the lace, and then tuck the lace over your belt with the knot inside under the belt. The knot won't slide out but can be pulled easily enough when you want to use the knife.

Overweight Dog Warning

If your dog is getting fat, you're probably not getting enough exercise. Take the dog for a walk.

Rubber Roofing Makes a Great Tarp

Old rubber roofing makes a durable waterproof tarp, and it can be scavenged for free from roofers who have to remove it to install new roofs. One side will be dirty but the other clean and new-looking. Brush and hose off the dirt, cut to size, and use it to cover a woodpile, four-wheeler, or whatever. Waterproof, heavier than a plastic tarp and will not deteriorate as rapidly. Holes are easily repaired with roofing patches.

Index

Symbols

M

N

P

R

S

NOTES

NOTES

NOTES

NOTES